# · *microwave* ·
# BAKING

# • *micro*wave •
# BAKING

*Traditional favourites for the contemporary cook*

• LINDA FRASER •

Macdonald Orbis

I would like to thank Sarah Barrass for her help in testing the recipes; Allan, my husband, and Coralie Dorman for their help and support; Felicity Jackson for her careful editing; Lakeland Plastics for providing all the microwave equipment for testing; and Toshiba for the loan of a microwave cooker.

A Macdonald Orbis Book

First published in Great Britain in 1989
by Macdonald & Co (Publishers) Ltd
London & Sydney

A member of Maxwell Pergamon Publishing Corporation plc



British Library Cataloguing in Publication Data
Fraser, Linda
Microwave baking.
1. Baking using microwave ovens. Recipes.
I. Title
641.7′1

ISBN 0-356-17165-5

Typeset by Bookworm Typesetting, Manchester
Printed and bound in Great Britain by Purnell Book Production Ltd

Illustrations by Robert McAulay

Editor: Coralie Dorman
Text Editor: Felicity Jackson
Senior Art Editor: Clive Hayball
Designer: David Rowley
Photographer: James Murphy
assisted by Rachel Andrew
Stylist: Sarah Wiley
Food For Photography: Linda Fraser
assisted by Sarah Barrass and Helen Corner

Macdonald & Co (Publishers) Ltd
Greater London House
Hampstead Road
London NW1 7QX

# CONTENTS

# INTRODUCTION

When I was first asked to plan this book, I secretly thought that finding nearly 150 recipes that baked well in a microwave was a bit of a tall order. However, I wrote out long lists of recipes that I liked cooking conventionally – the list included cakes and custard-filled flans, soft rolls, whisked sponges, cheesecakes and biscuits (to name but a few!) and to be honest, I suspected that a lot of the ideas wouldn't work. However, as the testing progressed and I tasted the results; I began to realise just how versatile the microwave cooker is.

For a variety of reasons there are a few traditionally baked foods that can't be cooked in a microwave – choux pastry doesn't set and falls flat as soon as microwaving stops; the pastry in double crust pies stays soggy (though pastry flan cases, cooked before the filling is added, work very well); cakes with a high proportion of sugar or dried fruit overheat and dry up; and traditional meringues either stay soft and sticky, or contain too much sugar and burn easily. But the vast majority of baking recipes work well, with the advantage that they almost all cook in a fraction of the time taken conventionally.

## ACHIEVING GOOD RESULTS

**Covering** Microwaves cook by agitating the molecules in the food, creating heat, which in turn produces steam. Microwaved food is usually covered to trap this steam which then keeps the food moist and speeds up the cooking process. However, the only microwave baked foods in this book to be covered in this way are sponge and suet puddings because conventionally they are steamed.

Cakes, biscuits and breads are cooked uncovered to let the outside surface dry.

Whether you cover the surface or not, cakes and breads cooked in a microwave stay too moist to form a brown crust, but this doesn't matter as much as you might think. Recipes can be adapted to include brown ingredients, such as wholewheat flour or spices, or the tops can be browned under a grill (this works especially well with breads and scones) and, of course, if a cake is to be iced or covered with cream the absence of a crust won't be noticed at all. In the recipes in this book dishes are uncovered unless otherwise specified. If covering, use a lid or an inverted plate. At the time of going to press it has been recommended that clingfilm should not be used for microwave cooking, as it has been found that some of the plasticiser used to soften clingfilm can transfer to the food during cooking.

**Timing** Unlike those cooked conventionally, microwaved cakes, breads and puddings continue cooking through to the centre for a short time after the cooker is switched off. The secret to successful baking is to always stop microwaving before the food is ready, then leave it to stand on a work surface to complete cooking. Working out just when to stop microwaving is a little tricky at first – cakes, biscuits and breads cook amazingly quickly (with many recipes taking less than 5 minutes) so the margins between under and overcooking are very small. However, once you recognise the tell-tale signs, getting good results becomes quite easy. Because microwaved cakes and breads keep cooking for a short time after they are removed from the cooker – they don't collapse if you switch off the power for a moment or two during cooking – it means that you can check them as often as needed. The exception is puff pastry which must be left until it sets before you open the door.

**What to Look For** After microwaving, biscuits and pastry should be dry on top, but still have a few moist spots on the base – these will dry on standing. If undercooked they will be chewy, and if overcooked they will be hard and tough.

Cakes and teabreads should be just starting to shrink from the sides of the dish and be almost dry on top. With deep cakes, check that the centre is cooked by inserting a fine skewer through to the base – it should come out clean. If you have judged the microwaving time right, there will still be a small moist spot in the centre of the base which will cook during standing time and show as a darker ring when the cake is turned out.

Cheesecakes and egg-based pie fillings cook round the outside first. Stop cooking them when all but a 5 cm/2 in central spot is set. This will cook by convected heat from the outside during standing. Microwaved cheesecakes are very soft after cooking, but firm up after chilling.

## TIPS FOR SUCCESS

Achieving good results doesn't just depend on your ability to judge the cooking time correctly – there are several other techniques that can make quite a difference.

**Add Extra Liquid** Adding extra liquid to cake and bread mixtures, makes them cook and rise more evenly and stay fresher. To convert conventional recipes, add 1–2 tbsp extra liquid in breads and the same amount per egg in cake mixtures, which need to be a very soft dropping consistency.

**Techniques for Pastry** To make pastry cases crisp, roll out thinly (to about 3 mm/⅛ in) and prick all over with a fork. Lay a double thickness of absorbent paper inside to absorb any excess moisture, then if you have some, fill with a layer of ceramic baking beans to keep the base flat and support the sides. These small grey beans look like round grey pebbles and are used instead of dried beans, the traditional weights for pastry cases, which can't be used because they absorb the microwave energy and burn.

**Use a Microwave Rack** All microwave bakes cook more evenly on a microwave rack, because it raises the dish off the floor of the cooker and lets the microwaves cook underneath too.

**Avoid Hot Spots** Some cookers have areas called hot spots that cook more quickly than the rest, causing cakes to rise unevenly or one of a number of smaller items to cook more quickly. Cooking is more even if the dish or tray is rotated all the time and a turntable does this job quite well. You may have to rotate individual items manually or rearrange them if some areas cook more quickly than others.

**Rotate the Dishes** If your cooker doesn't have a turntable, you will have to rotate the dishes by hand, giving them a quarter turn at least 3 times during cooking. Some of the recipes in this book call for a rectangular dish that is too large to rotate automatically, and you will have to either remove or switch off the turntable (if in accordance with the manufacturer's instructions) and rotate the dish manually.

**Cook in Circles** The centre of cakes, breads and desserts is usually last to cook because, for various reasons, less microwave energy reaches the centre of the cooker and in large cakes the middle can stay obstinately raw while the outside starts to overcook; the problem is solved by using a ring dish.

Small items like buns, cakes and biscuits are always arranged in a circle so that they cook evenly – do not place one in the centre because, just like the centre of a cake, it will cook more slowly than the rest.

## TURNING OUT

Microwaved cakes are especially soft and fragile when they are first turned out. Always turn the cake out on to your hand and then invert it on to the wire rack to cool. This way the top doesn't become marked by or stick to the rack. For very soft cakes, you should also cover the rack with a clean tea towel to prevent the base sinking into the rack. It is a good idea to cover cakes and bread with a tea towel while they cool as this keeps them soft and moist.

## SUGARY MIXTURES

It has been suggested that high sugar foods such as caramel or praline are best cooked conventionally. They are a little tricky to microwave, but as long as you take the necessary care, you'll find they are much easier by microwave.

Sugary foods become extremely hot so when handling them you must be extra careful. Always cook them in heatproof glass and, as hot mixtures heat their containers, use oven gloves!

Never leave a sugar mixture unattended while cooking, even if you've cooked the same recipe before, as slight changes in the quantities or temperature of the food can alter the cooking time. Remember also that the mixture will continue to cook after you switch off the microwave.

## HOW LONG DOES IT KEEP?

The keeping qualities of microwave baked food depend largely on good cooking.

**Breads and Cakes** Unless they contain moist ingredients like onion or cheese, breads are best eaten warm, fresh from the cooker. To keep breads and cakes as moist as possible, turn them out on to a wire rack covered with a tea towel, keep covered until cool, then wrap tightly in foil. If the cooled cake or bread is still soft and spongy, it will keep for a day or two at least. Cakes also keep better if they are iced or covered with cream.

**Biscuits and Pastry** Biscuits and pastries keep very well for 2–3 days in an airtight container and can be refreshed by microwaving on a plastic rack for a short time (cover the rack with absorbent paper first to help them crisp up).

**Cheesecakes** The texture of cheesecakes improves after cooling and if kept in a cool place they are very good the next day.

## FREEZING

Butter cream-filled cakes, sponge puddings, breads and biscuits all freeze quite well, but they tend to dry out if frozen for more than a month. Defrost at room temperature – filled cakes will take 2–3 hours, biscuits and pastry about 30 minutes – 1 hour. Thawed plain cakes, breads and biscuits can be microwaved again for a short time to warm them through. To keep biscuits and pastry from becoming soggy, microwave on a rack lined with a double layer of absorbent paper.

## EQUIPMENT

Traditional baking dishes are almost all metal and these must not be used in the microwave, so if you are going to try microwave baking you may need to buy some new dishes. For this book, I've kept the range of microwave dishes quite small, and I've tried to use the same shape for several different recipes. You may find that you already have dishes that are the right shape for some of the recipes. For instance, a round glass pizza dish makes an excellent baking tray and glass or china soufflé dishes are good cake dishes.

When I was testing the recipes, I used plastic microwave dishes for all the actual baking processes. These dishes are specially designed for microwaving and, as well as being microwave transparent (ie they allow microwaves to pass through very quickly), they are relatively non-stick. The best ones also have a number of other features that make them good for microwave baking: sloping sides, rounded corners, a transparent base (so you can see when pastry or cakes are cooked), and handles.

One of the most useful cake dishes available has 2 transparent, loose bases – one flat and one which neatly converts the dish to a ring shape. The loose base has an added advantage, it makes turning out the cake very easy. Loose-based flan dishes are particularly good for the same reason. These hard plastic dishes are quite expensive, but are very durable and well worth buying if you intend to do a lot of baking.

The cheaper, flexible plastic dishes are ideal for most microwave baking; they have most of the same good points as hard plastic dishes but don't last as long. Their biggest drawback is that they soften as they heat up so larger dishes need to be supported on a glass or hard plastic baking tray, to prevent them twisting when you remove them from the microwave. They must not be used for very sugary or fatty foods which can get hot enough to melt the plastic.

**Choosing the Best Shape** Because of the way microwaves work, the shape of the dish affects the cooking results. You can cook in any shape; round dishes and especially ring dishes cook most evenly, but sandwich dishes, because they are so shallow, come a close second; and small round or square dishes and wide, shallow loaf dishes are all almost as good.

Loaf dishes are used quite a lot in conventional baking because the finished product cuts into such neat slices, but they are probably the worst shape for microwaving. The ends and especially the corners get a double dose of microwave energy so cook much more quickly than the middle. You can offset this effect to some extent by sticking small strips of foil on to the corners of the dish for about half the cooking time to shield them from the microwaves. However, I find that a slightly wider and shallower loaf shape works very well – without shielding.

A concave base (like the bottom of a bowl) lets the microwaves reach the deepest part of a cake, so pudding basins and mixing bowls are a good choice for more slowly cooked fruit cakes.

## THE POWER SETTING PROBLEM

There isn't a standard power output, or number and name of settings which microwave manufacturers use and, unfortunately, some use the same terminology for completely different settings.

I tested all the recipes in a Toshiba microwave with a 650 watt output and used only 4 of the 9 settings for the recipes in this book:

HIGH or No 9 (100% power, 650 watts)
MEDIUM or No 5 (60% power, 390 watts)
DEFROST or No 3 (35% power, 230 watts)
LOW or No 1 (10% power, 65 watts)

The wording or numbering system in your microwave cooker may be different – check the power of your settings (you will find the information in your microwave handbook) and use the setting with the nearest equivalent power output. If your microwave has a different power than the one used in the recipes, you will need to recalculate the cooking time.

The temperature of the kitchen and the ingredients have a marked effect on the baking times and results. In cold weather, cakes and breads won't rise as much and will take longer to cook than in summer when cakes rise wonderfully and may take considerably less time to cook. Don't forget, the cooking time is only a guide -- always check during cooking and stop when the food is ready rather than when the time is up.

**Adjusting Cooking Times** Ovens with a power output of 700 watts may cook slightly quicker, so cook the recipe for slightly less time than suggested, checking carefully during the second half of the cooking time. For 600 or 500 watt microwaves, first cook for the time suggested, then if necessary cook for a little longer.

The cooking time is also affected by the size of the cooker cavity but as high power cookers tend to be large, and low powered cookers quite small you may find that you won't have to adjust the time very much.

## MEASUREMENTS

Use either metric or imperial measurements, don't switch from one to another in the same recipe.

This section contains lots of delicious, sliceable cakes for eating every day. There are familiar favourites like gingerbread, cream-filled sponges and Swiss roll as well as some interesting new ideas and flavour combinations which I hope you will try. Some of the most inspiring ideas come from abroad – especially Australia and America – where sour cream, coconut, chocolate and even grated vegetables are popular cake ingredients.

When I'm baking (either conventionally or by microwave) I like to use the traditional creaming method – beating the butter and sugar together first, then beating in the eggs and finally folding in the flour. Cakes made this way always turn out lighter, are less dry and have a soft, even texture. Most of the sponge recipes suggest this method. First soften the butter, then add the other ingredients with an extra pinch of baking powder and beat together.

There are countless ways of improving the looks of microwaved cakes – from a single dusting of sugar to a more elaborate frosting or icing, and several of the recipes have baked-on toppings that give the cooked cakes an appetizing appearance.

Even if you are a beginner baker, I'm sure you will find the recipes in this chapter very simple to make.

CHAPTER ONE

# FAMILY CAKES

## NEAPOLITAN CAKE

◆

175 g/6 oz butter
175 g/6 oz self-raising flour
175 g/6 oz caster sugar
3 eggs, beaten
1 tsp vanilla essence
5 tbsp milk
few drops of pink food colouring
4 tsp cocoa powder, sifted
3 tbsp apricot jam
1 quantity Crème au Beurre (see p. 122)
1 quantity Glacé Icing (see p. 114)

◆

1 Grease and base-line three 9 × 18 cm/3½ × 7 in loaf dishes.
2 Put the butter in a mixing bowl and cook on HIGH for 25 seconds to soften.
3 Sift the flour into the bowl, then add the sugar, eggs, vanilla essence and 4 tbsp of the milk. Beat the mixture until well blended, smooth and light.
4 Divide the mixture into 3; leave 1 portion plain, mix a few drops of colouring into the second portion to make it pale pink, and add the cocoa and the remaining milk to the third.
5 Spoon the mixtures into separate dishes and spread evenly. Cook (one at a time) on HIGH for 1½–2 minutes, or until just beginning to shrink from the sides.
6 Leave the cakes to stand for 5 minutes, then turn out on to a wire rack to cool. Sandwich the cakes with apricot jam and place on a serving plate.
7 Reserve 4 tbsp of the crème au beurre for piping. Spread the rest over the sides of the cake using a serrated edge scraper.
8 Pipe shells around the top and bottom edges of the cake with the reserved crème au beurre.
9 Make the glacé icing; for feathering, the icing shouldn't be too thin, so add the water drop by drop until the icing is just wet enough to find its own level in the bowl. Colour 1 tbsp of the icing pink in a separate bowl, and add the cocoa and a little extra water to another 1 tbsp in a third bowl.
10 Coat the top of the cake with the plain icing, then drizzle the coloured icings on top in 6 or 8 alternate lines the length of the cake. Quickly draw a skewer across the piped lines, first in one direction, then in the other to make a feather pattern. Leave for 30 minutes, then cut into 12 slices.

## DATE AND APPLE CAKE

◆

115 g/4 oz chopped dates
6 tbsp milk
115 g/4 oz butter
115 g/4 oz caster sugar
2 eggs, beaten
115 g/4 oz self-raising flour, sifted
1 cooking apple, peeled, cored and chopped
2 tbsp demerara sugar

◆

1 Grease and base-line a 15 × 23 cm/6 × 9 in cake dish.
2 Put the dates and milk in a small bowl, cover and cook on HIGH for 3 minutes, then stir and leave to cool. Put the butter in a mixing bowl and cook on HIGH for 20 seconds to soften. Add the sugar and beat until light and fluffy.
3 Beat in the eggs a little at a time, beating well after each addition. Add the flour and fold into the creamed mixture with the date mixture and the apple.
4 Spoon the cake mixture into the dish and smooth the surface. Cook on HIGH for 3 minutes, then sprinkle with half of the demerara sugar and cook on HIGH for 5 minutes, or until springy to touch. Sprinkle with the remaining sugar and leave to stand for 5 minutes. Turn out and cool on a wire rack. Cut into 15 squares.

## CREAM-FILLED SPONGE CAKE

*During cooking, the sponge rises to about twice its original depth then falls back slightly. Make sure that the dish is greased right to the top to prevent the cake sticking or it will break round the top edge.*

175 g/6 oz butter
75 g/3 oz self-raising flour
75 g/3 oz wholewheat self-raising flour
175 g/6 oz caster sugar
3 eggs, beaten
4 tbsp milk
4 tbsp raspberry jam
150 ml/¼ pint double cream, whipped
icing sugar, to dust

1 Grease and base-line a deep 20 cm/8 in round cake dish.
2 Put the butter in a mixing bowl and cook on HIGH for 25 seconds to soften.
3 Sift the flours into the bowl, tipping in any bran caught in the sieve, then add the sugar, eggs and milk.
4 Beat until the mixture is well blended, smooth and light, then spoon into the cake dish and spread evenly.
5 Cook on HIGH for 5½–6 minutes, or until just beginning to shrink from the sides of the dish.
6 Leave to stand for 5 minutes, then turn out on to a wire rack to cool.
7 Split the cake horizontally and sandwich together with the jam and cream. Dust the top with icing sugar and cut into 8 wedges.

## CHERRY AND ALMOND CAKE

*This buttery cherry cake looks very pretty with its colourful topping of chopped cherries and toasted almonds.*

150 g/5 oz butter
150 g/5 oz light soft brown sugar
few drops of almond essence
50 g/2 oz ground almonds
2 eggs, beaten
115 g/4 oz wholewheat flour, sifted
2 tbsp milk
75 g/3 oz glacé cherries, washed, dried and quartered
15 g/½ oz flaked almonds, toasted (see p. 120)

1 Grease and base-line a deep 20 cm/8 in round cake dish.
2 Put the butter in a mixing bowl and cook on HIGH for 20 seconds to soften. Add the sugar and almond essence and beat until light and fluffy.
3 Beat in the ground almonds, then the eggs a little at a time, beating well after each addition. Fold in the flour with the milk and 50 g/2 oz of the cherries.
4 Spoon into the prepared dish and spread evenly. Cook on HIGH for 3 minutes, then sprinkle with the flaked almonds and reserved cherries. Cook for a further 3½–4 minutes, or until the cake begins to shrink from the sides of the dish.
5 Leave the cake to stand for 5 minutes, then turn out on to a wire rack to cool. Cut into 8 wedges.

# CHOCOLATE RIPPLE RING

*Ring dishes are an ideal shape for microwave baking because the centre, which usually takes longest to cook, isn't there! So the whole cake cooks very evenly and keeps beautifully moist. This one has a little cocoa mixture stirred in to give a rippled effect to the sponge when it is sliced.*

◆

175 g/6 oz butter
200 g/7 oz caster sugar
3 eggs, beaten
200 g/7 oz self-raising flour, sifted
5 tbsp milk
2 tbsp cocoa powder, sifted
½ quantity Chocolate Fudge Frosting (see p. 116)

◆

1 Grease and base-line a 20 cm/8 in ring dish.
2 Put the butter in a mixing bowl and cook on HIGH for 25 seconds to soften. Add the sugar and beat until light and fluffy. Add the eggs a little at a time, beating well after each addition, then fold in the flour and 2 tbsp of the milk.
3 Mix the cocoa with the remaining milk, then add 2 tbsp of the cake mixture and blend together. Stir the chocolate mixture into the cake mixture to give a rippled effect and spoon into the prepared dish.
4 Cook on HIGH for 5–6 minutes, or until just shrinking from the sides of the dish. Leave to stand for 5 minutes, then turn out on to a wire rack to cool.
5 Make the frosting and spread over the cake with a palette knife. Leave to set for 30 minutes, then cut into 12 slices.

From left to right: Chocolate ripple ring, Neapolitan cake page 12, Cherry and almond cake page 13

## Speckled Swiss Roll

*If you don't have a cake dish the right size, use 2 or 3 layers of baking parchment, fold in the edges to form 2.5 cm/1 in high walls and fix the corners with sticky tape.*

◆

4 eggs, separated
150 g/5 oz caster sugar
2 tbsp hot water
50 g/2 oz plain dessert chocolate, grated
75 g/3 oz self-raising flour, sifted twice
150 ml/¼ pint double cream
2 tsp icing sugar
1 tsp vanilla essence

◆

1 Line a shallow 20 × 30 cm/8 × 12 in dish with baking parchment.
2 Beat the egg yolks and 115 g/4 oz of the caster sugar over a bowl of hot water with an electric beater for about 5 minutes until the mixture will hold the trail from the beaters for nearly 10 seconds.
3 Whisk the egg whites in a separate bowl with clean beaters until holding soft peaks.
4 Fold the water and chocolate into the yolk mixture, then the flour and the whites.
5 Pour the mixture into the prepared dish and gently smooth the surface. Cook on HIGH for 5½–6 minutes, or until well risen and still slightly damp on the surface. Leave to stand for 3 minutes.
6 Place a sheet of baking parchment on the work surface and sprinkle with the remaining caster sugar. Turn the sponge out on top of the sugared paper. Remove the lining paper and trim the edges of the sponge.
7 Lay another sheet of baking parchment on top and loosely roll up from a short end. Leave to cool.
8 Pour the cream into a bowl, add the icing sugar and vanilla essence and whip until holding soft peaks. Unroll the sponge, spread with cream and re-roll. Dust with more caster sugar and cut into 8 slices.

## Chocolate Sandwich Cake

*This sponge is flavoured with plain chocolate instead of the usual cocoa and is filled with a creamy white frosting. To prevent stray dark crumbs getting into the frosting and spoiling the appearance, spread the cake with a thin first layer of frosting to seal, then finish with the rest of the frosting.*

◆

175 g/6 oz butter
75 g/3 oz plain chocolate
3 tbsp milk
115 g/4 oz plain flour
2 tsp baking powder
50 g/2 oz cocoa powder
175 g/6 oz light soft brown sugar
3 eggs, beaten
1 quantity Vanilla Fast Frosting (see p. 117)

◆

1 Grease and base-line two 19 cm/7½ in round cake dishes.
2 Put the butter in a mixing bowl and cook on HIGH for 25 seconds to soften.
3 Break the chocolate into squares and place in a small bowl with the milk. Cook on MEDIUM for 3–4 minutes to melt.
4 Meanwhile, sift together the flour, baking powder and cocoa into the mixing bowl. Add the sugar, eggs and chocolate.
5 Beat the mixture until it is well blended, smooth and light. Divide it between the cake dishes and spread evenly.
6 Cook the cakes (one at a time) on HIGH for 2–2½ minutes, until just beginning to shrink from the sides of the dish. Leave the cakes to stand for 5 minutes, then turn out on to a wire rack to cool.
7 Make the frosting and use some to sandwich the cakes. Spread the rest over the top and sides of the cake with a palette knife, leaving the surface rough. Leave to set for 10 minutes, then cut into 8 wedges.

## SOURED CREAM SPICE CAKE

*Soured cream not only adds a pleasant tangy taste to cakes, but also makes them extra light and spongy. This cake has crunchy layers of walnuts, cinnamon and sugar cooked in the middle and on top.*

◆

125 g/4½ oz butter
½ tsp vanilla essence
75 g/3 oz caster sugar
1 egg, beaten
150 ml/¼ pint soured cream
2 tbsp milk
115 g/4 oz plain flour
40 g/1½ oz wholewheat self-raising flour
½ tsp bicarbonate of soda
1½ tsp ground cinnamon
75 g/3 oz chopped walnuts
2 tbsp light soft brown sugar

◆

1 Grease and base-line a deep 20 cm/8 in round cake dish.
2 Put the butter in a mixing bowl and cook on HIGH for 20 seconds to soften. Add the vanilla essence and caster sugar and beat until light and fluffy. Beat in the egg a little at a time; stir in the soured cream and milk.
3 Sift the flours, bicarbonate of soda and ½ tsp of the cinnamon into the bowl, tipping in any bran caught in the sieve. Stir the mixture until well blended.
4 Spread half of the cake mixture in the dish. Mix the walnuts, brown sugar and remaining cinnamon together and scatter half over the cake mixture in the dish.
5 Spoon the rest of the cake mixture on top and smooth the surface before scattering over the remaining walnut mixture.
6 Cook on HIGH for 6 minutes, or until just shrinking from sides of dish. Leave to stand for 5 minutes, then turn out on to a wire rack to cool. Cut into 8 wedges.

## BANANA AND BRAZIL CAKE

*Bananas add a moist sweetness to this cake. Use ripe yellow bananas as they are much sweeter than the firmer green-tinged ones.*

◆

150 g/5 oz butter
150 g/5 oz caster sugar
2 eggs plus 1 yolk, beaten
2 bananas (about 75 g/3 oz each), mashed
115 g/4 oz shelled Brazil nuts
200 g/7 oz self-raising flour, sifted
2 tsp apricot jam
icing sugar, to dust
225 g/8 oz marzipan

◆

1 Grease and line a 900 g/2 lb loaf dish.
2 Put the butter in a mixing bowl and cook on HIGH for 20 seconds to soften. Add the sugar and beat until light and fluffy. Beat in the eggs a little at a time, then stir in the bananas.
3 Reserve 3 or 4 of the Brazil nuts for the decoration and coarsely chop the rest. Stir into the mixture with the flour.
4 Spoon into the prepared dish and smooth the surface. Cook on HIGH for 7 minutes, or until a skewer inserted into the centre comes out clean. Leave to stand for 10 minutes, then turn out on to a wire rack to cool.
5 Put the jam in a small bowl and cook on HIGH for 15–30 seconds to soften, then brush over the top of the cake. Dust a board with icing sugar and roll out the marzipan to fit the top of the cake. Press it on to the top and mark a lattice on the surface with a knife.
6 Cut the reserved Brazil nuts into small chunks and press one into each square of the lattice. Brown the marzipan under a hot grill (watch it carefully as it browns very quickly). Cut into 12 slices.

From top to bottom: Golden ginger cake, German lattice loaf, Banana and brazil cake page 17

## GERMAN LATTICE LOAF

*The original rather interesting idea for this cake came from Germany. The cake itself is full of fruit, crunchy nuts and seeds, and on top has a thick lattice of plain cake that is brushed with apricot glaze. The recipe converts to microwaving well and it cooks amazingly quickly – taking just 2½ minutes on High.*

◆

2 tbsp milk
25 g/1 oz sesame seeds
2 tsp poppy seeds
25 g/1 oz sultanas
50 g/ 2 oz glacé cherries, chopped
25 g/1 oz caster sugar
1 egg yolk
115 g/4 oz self-raising flour
pinch of salt
40 g/1½ oz butter
40 g/1½ oz light soft brown sugar
1 egg, beaten
2 tbsp hot water
1 tbsp apricot jam

◆

1 Grease and line a 900 g/2 lb loaf dish.
2 Pour the milk into a small jug and add the sesame and poppy seeds. Cook on HIGH for 2–3 minutes until the milk is absorbed. Stir in the sultanas, cherries, caster sugar and egg yolk and set aside.
3 Sift the flour and salt into a bowl, then rub in the butter until the mixture resembles breadcrumbs. Stir in the brown sugar and mix to a soft dough with the egg and water.
4 Spoon about four-fifths of the mixture into the prepared dish and spread evenly. Sprinkle the seed mixture over the top and press gently with the back of a spoon.
5 Place the remaining cake mixture in a piping bag fitted with a 5 mm/¼ in plain nozzle and pipe a diagonal lattice over the filling.
6 Cook on HIGH for 2½ minutes, or until just beginning to shrink from the sides of the dish. Leave to stand for 5 minutes, then turn out on to a wire rack. Warm the jam on HIGH for 30 seconds, then brush over the lattice and filling. Leave to cool, then cut into 12 slices.

## GOLDEN GINGER CAKE

*Quite unlike a traditional ginger cake, this light coloured sponge is subtly flavoured with lemon and fresh ginger.*

◆

175 g/6 oz butter
175 g/6 oz dark soft brown sugar
175 g/6 oz plain flour
1½ tsp baking powder
5 cm/2 in piece fresh root ginger, peeled and finely grated
3 eggs, beaten
grated rind and juice of 1 lemon
½ quantity Lemon Crème au Beurre (see p. 122)
1–2 pieces stem ginger, cut into thin slivers

◆

1 Grease and base-line a deep 20 cm/8 in round cake dish.
2 Put the butter in a mixing bowl and cook on HIGH for 25 seconds to soften. Beat in the sugar. Sift in the flour and baking powder, then add the fresh ginger, eggs and lemon rind and juice. Beat together until well blended, light and fluffy.
3 Spoon the mixture into the prepared dish and smooth the surface. Cook on HIGH for 7 minutes, or until cake begins to shrink from the sides of the dish. Leave the cake to stand for 5 minutes before turning out on to a wire rack to cool.
4 Make the crème au beurre, spread over the top of the cake and scatter with the slivers of ginger. Cut into 8 wedges.

# COCONUT AND HONEY LOAF

*Coconut and honey complement each other perfectly in this cake. The coconut keeps it moist and gives the overall taste, while the honey as well as being a natural sweetener imparts a delicate flavour of its own – especially, if you use a scented honey such as orange blossom or heather.*

50 g/2 oz butter
75 g/3 oz light soft brown sugar
1 egg, beaten
115 g/4 oz self-raising flour, sifted
2 tbsp honey
115 g/4 oz desiccated coconut, toasted (see p. 120)
50 ml/2 fl oz milk

1 Grease and line a 900 g/2 lb loaf dish.
2 Put the butter in a mixing bowl and cook on HIGH for 15 seconds to soften. Add the sugar, egg, flour, 1 tbsp of the honey, 50 g/2 oz of the coconut and the milk. Beat until well blended.
3 Spoon into the prepared dish and smooth the surface. Mix the remaining honey and coconut together and spread over the cake mixture.
4 Cook on HIGH for 4 minutes, or until the mixture begins to shrink from the sides of the dish. Leave to stand for 3 minutes, then turn out and cool on a wire rack. Cut into 12 slices.

# COCONUT MACAROON CAKE

*A whipped egg white, coconut and almond mixture is spread over this cake partway through cooking to form a thick soft topping. It is possible to turn out the cake from an ordinary dish (without spoiling the topping) by carefully inverting it on to a board or tray and then back on to a rack. However, a dish with a loose bottom makes the job a lot easier – place the loose-bottomed dish on a slightly smaller bowl, let the outside ring drop down and then, just lift off the cake.*

115 g/4 oz butter
grated rind of 1 lemon
115 g/4 oz caster sugar
2 eggs, separated
150 g/5 oz self-raising flour, sifted
75 g/3 oz ground almonds
120 ml/4 fl oz milk
25 g/1 oz light soft brown sugar
75 g/3 oz desiccated coconut, toasted (see p. 120)

1 Grease and line a deep 20 cm/8 in loose-bottomed ring dish.
2 Put the butter in a mixing bowl and cook on HIGH for 20 seconds to soften. Add the lemon rind, caster sugar, egg yolks, flour, 50 g/2 oz of the almonds and the milk and mix thoroughly. Spoon the mixture into the prepared dish and cook on HIGH for 5 minutes.
3 While the cake is cooking, whisk the egg whites in a separate bowl until they form soft peaks. Fold in the soft brown sugar, the remaining almonds and all but 1 tbsp of the coconut.
4 Quickly spoon this mixture over the hot cake and spread evenly. Sprinkle with the reserved coconut and cook on MEDIUM for 3–4 minutes, until the topping is set. Leave to stand for 5 minutes, then turn out on to a wire rack to cool. Cut into 10 slices.

## PARKIN

*Microwaved Parkin has a tendency to be dry, so I've added apricots and sultanas to the mixture. Spread the slices with butter or, as suggested in an old recipe book of mine, serve it with wedges of cheese.*

115 g/4 oz dried apricots, finely chopped
50 g/2 oz sultanas
75 g/3 oz butter
3 tbsp black treacle
40 g/1 ½ oz dark soft brown sugar
175 g/6 oz wholewheat flour
½ tsp salt
½ tsp bicarbonate of soda
½ tsp baking powder
1 ½ tsp ground ginger
175 g/6 oz medium oatmeal
50 ml/2 fl oz milk
2 eggs, beaten

1 Grease and base-line a deep 15 × 23 cm/6 × 9 in dish.
2 Put the apricots and sultanas in a bowl with 9 tbsp boiling water. Cover and cook on HIGH for 4 minutes, then leave to cool.
3 Put the butter, treacle and sugar in a small bowl and cook on HIGH for 2 minutes to melt, then stir to dissolve the sugar. Leave to cool.
4 Sift the flour, salt, bicarbonate of soda, baking powder and ginger into a mixing bowl, add the bran from the sieve and the oatmeal.
5 Add the cooled fruit, the melted mixture, and the milk and eggs. Mix thoroughly. Pour into the prepared dish and cook on HIGH for 8–10 minutes, until a skewer inserted into the centre comes out clean.
6 Leave the parkin to stand for 15 minutes, then turn out on to a wire rack to cool. Cut in half lengthways, then across into 20 slices.

## STICKY GINGERBREAD

*Unlike most microwaved cakes, gingerbread keeps very well as long as it is kept tightly wrapped in foil. In fact the texture and flavour definitely improve after a day or so – and even after 3 or 4 days the gingerbread will still be deliciously moist. Slice it thickly and spread with butter – it's the kind of cake you can eat at any time of day.*

75 g/3 oz butter
175 g/6 oz black treacle
50 g/2 oz dark soft brown sugar
120 ml/4 fl oz milk
½ tsp bicarbonate of soda
175 g/6 oz wholewheat self-raising flour
2 tsp ground ginger
¼ tsp mixed spice
1 egg, beaten

1 Grease and line a 900 g/2 lb loaf dish.
2 Put the butter, treacle and sugar in a mixing bowl and cook on HIGH for 2½ minutes, then stir to dissolve the sugar. Leave to cool slightly, then stir in the milk and bicarbonate of soda.
3 Sift together the flour, ginger and mixed spice and add to the melted mixture with the bran from the sieve. Add the egg and mix until smooth.
4 Pour the mixture into the prepared dish and cook on MEDIUM-HIGH for 8–10 minutes, or until a skewer inserted into the centre comes out clean.
5 Leave to stand for 5 minutes, then turn out on to a wire rack to cool. Cut into 12 slices.

## Marmalade Spice Cake

*Spice cakes have much more flavour if you freshly grind or grate the spices rather than buying them ready ground. When you store them, the whole spices keep their flavour longer than the ready ground ones. However, if you have only ground spices the flavour should still be alright, as long as the jars have not been languishing in your store cupboard for years.*

◆

115 g/4 oz butter
50 g/2 oz light soft brown sugar
2 tbsp golden syrup
2 eggs, beaten
9 tbsp orange marmalade
225 g/8 oz self-raising flour
½ tsp grated nutmeg
½ tsp ground cinnamon
¼ tsp ground cloves
150 ml/¼ pint milk
2 oranges, peeled and sliced

◆

**1** Grease and base-line a deep 15 × 23 cm/6 × 9 in cake dish.
**2** Put the butter in a mixing bowl and cook on HIGH for 20 seconds to soften. Add the sugar and golden syrup and beat until light and fluffy. Beat in the eggs a little at a time, beating well after each addition.
**3** Stir in 3 tbsp of the marmalade. Sift together the flour and spices and fold into the cake mixture with the milk.
**4** Spoon into the prepared dish and smooth the surface. Cook on HIGH for 7 minutes, or until a skewer pushed into the centre comes out clean. Leave to stand for 5 minutes, then turn out on to a wire rack to cool.
**5** Put the remaining marmalade in a small bowl and cook on HIGH for 1–1½ minutes to melt. Brush a little over the cake. Arrange the orange slices all over, overlapping them slightly, then brush with the rest of the warm marmalade. Leave to set for 10 minutes, then cut into 20 slices.

## Fruit Salad Sponge

*A mixture of fresh, dried and glacé fruits make this sponge moist and sweet. To make the flavour really tangy, cook the citrus fruits on* HIGH *for 30 seconds before squeezing – you'll get much more juice when they are warm. The frosting isn't essential as the cake is also good sliced and spread with butter.*

◆

75 g/3 oz butter
grated rind and juice of ½ lemon
grated rind and juice of ½ orange
75 g/3 oz caster sugar
2 eggs, beaten
150 g/5 oz self-raising flour, sifted
75 g/3 oz pre-soaked dried apricots, chopped
40 g/1½ oz glacé cherries, chopped
1 eating apple, peeled, cored and chopped
½ quantity Orange Fast Frosting (see p. 117)

◆

**1** Grease and base-line a 9 × 20 cm/3½ × 8 in loaf dish.
**2** Put the butter in a mixing bowl and cook on HIGH for 15–20 seconds to soften. Add the lemon and orange rind and sugar, then beat the mixture until light and fluffy.
**3** Beat in the eggs a little at a time with a sprinkling of flour. Fold in the rest of the flour with the fruit juices and the fruit.
**4** Spoon the mixture into the dish and spread evenly, then cook on HIGH for 3½–4 minutes, until a skewer inserted into the centre comes out clean.
**5** Leave to stand for 5 minutes, then turn out and cool on a wire rack. Make the frosting and spread on top of the cake. Leave to set for 10 minutes before cutting into 12 slices.

From top to bottom: Marmalade spice cake, Sticky gingerbread page 21, Fruit salad sponge

## TOFFEE RAISIN CAKE

*The flavours of the butter, brown sugar and syrup blend together to give this cake a wonderful toffee taste. It's full of raisins too, but these can make the cake dry if it is cooked too long so check the centre of the cake with a skewer near the end of cooking time – if it comes out clean, the cake is ready.*

◆

150 g/5 oz butter
215 g/7½ oz light soft brown sugar
1 tbsp golden syrup
2 eggs, beaten
4 tbsp milk
190 g/6½ oz wholewheat self-raising flour, sifted
115 g/4 oz raisins
50 g/2 oz toasted chopped hazelnuts

◆

1 Grease and base-line a deep 20 cm/8 in round cake dish.
2 Put 90 g/3½ oz of the butter in a bowl and cook on HIGH for 20 seconds. Add 175 g/6 oz of the sugar, the syrup, eggs, milk and all but 1 tbsp of the flour and beat until light and fluffy.
3 Stir in three-quarters of the raisins, then spoon into the prepared dish. Spread evenly and cook on HIGH for 3 minutes. Meanwhile, add the hazelnuts to the remaining butter, sugar, flour and raisins. Rub together with your fingertips to form a crumbly mixture.
4 Sprinkle over the partly cooked cake and cook on HIGH for a further 3–4 minutes, until the topping is cooked and the cake begins to shrink from the sides of the dish.
5 Leave to stand for 5 minutes, then turn out on to a wire rack to cool. Cut into 8 wedges.

## FAMILY SPONGE CAKE

*This really is a quick family cake, it can be made from start to finish in about an hour, but it doesn't keep very well and should be eaten on the day it is made. The plain sponge is sandwiched and covered with Crème au Beurre and can be decorated with icing – use a ½ quantity of Glacé Icing (see p. 114) to pipe a decorative pattern on top, if wished.*

◆

175 g/6 oz butter
175 g/6 oz light soft brown sugar
3 eggs, beaten
175 g/6 oz self-raising flour, sifted
3 tbsp milk
1 quantity Crème au Beurre (see p. 122)

◆

1 Grease and base-line 2 deep 20 cm/8 in round dishes.
2 Put the butter in a mixing bowl and cook on HIGH for 25 seconds to soften. Beat in the sugar until light and fluffy, then beat in the eggs a little at a time, beating well after each addition.
3 Fold in the flour and milk until well blended. Divide the mixture between the dishes and spread evenly. Cook (one at a time) on HIGH for 4–4½ minutes, until springy to the touch. Leave to stand for 5 minutes, then turn out on to a wire rack to cool.
4 Make the butter cream (colour it if liked), then use one-third to sandwich the cakes together. Reserve 6 tbsp for piping and spread the rest over the top and sides of the cakes.
5 Put the reserved butter cream in a piping bag fitted with a star nozzle and pipe shells round the top and bottom edges. Cut into 12–16 wedges.

## COURGETTE AND CARROT CAKE

*Leave the skin on the courgette, it gives a delightful speckled effect to the sponge.*

◆

115 g/4 oz carrots, peeled and coarsely grated
115 g/4 oz courgettes, trimmed and coarsely grated
120 ml/4 fl oz vegetable oil
115 g/4 oz light soft brown sugar
2 tbsp clear honey
2 eggs, beaten
115 g/4 oz plain flour
115 g/4 oz wholewheat flour
1 tsp bicarbonate of soda
pinch of salt
2 tsp ground cinnamon
½ tsp grated nutmeg
1 quantity Orange Fromage Frais Frosting (see p. 117)

◆

1 Grease and base-line a deep 20 cm/8 in cake dish.
2 Put the carrots, courgettes, oil, sugar, honey and eggs in a mixing bowl and mix well. Sift together the flours, bicarbonate of soda, salt, cinnamon and nutmeg and add to the carrot mixture, tipping in any bran caught in the sieve.
3 Stir the mixture to blend all the ingredients together. Spoon into the prepared dish and smooth the surface.
4 Cook on HIGH for 7 minutes, or until a skewer inserted into the centre comes out clean. Leave to stand in the dish for 5 minutes, then turn out on to a wire rack to cool. Make the frosting while the cake is cooling, then spread on top and leave to set for about 30 minutes before cutting into 8 wedges.

## CRUNCHY-TOPPED CARDAMOM CAKE

*This cake has a wonderful scented smell from the cardamom. Use the seeds from white, green or black cardamom pods and grind them in a pestle and mortar just before you put them into the flour. This way you capture all the fragrance.*

◆

175 g/6 oz self-raising flour
2 tsp ground cardamom
115 g/4 oz butter, diced
175 g/6 oz light soft brown sugar
grated rind of 1 lemon
1 egg, beaten
150 ml/¼ pint natural yogurt
25 g/1 oz cornflakes, crushed

◆

1 Grease and base-line a deep 18 cm/7 in round cake dish.
2 Sift the flour and cardamom into a mixing bowl. Rub in the butter until the mixture resembles find breadcrumbs, then stir in the sugar and lemon rind.
3 Set aside 75 g/3 oz of the mixture for the topping. Add the egg and yogurt to the remaining mixture and mix thoroughly. Spoon the mixture into the prepared dish and smooth the surface.
4 Mix the cornflakes with the reserved crumb mixture and sprinkle over the cake mixture; press down gently with your hand.
5 Cook on HIGH for 5–6 minutes, until a skewer inserted into the centre comes out clean. Leave to stand for 5 minutes, then turn out on to a wire rack to cool. Cut into 8 wedges.

There's a wonderful range of small cakes and pastries that can be cooked successfully in the microwave – from plain scones or cup cakes to fondant-iced sponges and layered puff pastry slices. Some are cooked as tray bakes and cut up after cooling, while others are cooked in individual dishes. You can put a variety of containers to good use – tea cups, ramekins or paper cups can all be used – but don't be tempted to use disposable plastic cups as they will melt with the heat of the mixture.

Plain cup cakes and scones are especially quick to cook and are delicious warm from the cooker. Two of the tray bakes, Chocolate and Coconut Crunch and Florentine Slices, are very easy to make and even a small child can lend a hand with the mixing; make sure there is a grown up on hand to take the finished dish out of the cooker because the dishes get very hot. Budding young bakers should also have no trouble making the Hazel Nutties, Apricot Buns and St Clements Cakes.

Little iced cakes and quick-mix tray bakes made without flour keep quite well for a day or two, but in the main these microwaved cakes are best eaten on the day they are made. For this reason I've kept the quantities quite small – you can easily double or treble the recipe if you need more and they are so quick to make that you can easily bake some fresh every day.

CHAPTER TWO

# SMALL CAKES AND PASTRIES

## ECCLES CAKES

*Traditionally these little cakes were made from the scraps from a pie, re-rolled and cut into thin rounds. They look very plain after microwaving, but are sprinkled with demerara sugar and browned and crisped under a hot grill.*

◆

225 g/8 oz packet puff pastry
40 g/1 ½ oz currants
25 g/1 oz mixed chopped peel
15 g/½ oz butter
25 g/1 oz demerara sugar
¼ tsp ground allspice

◆

1 Place a double layer of absorbent paper on a microwave rack.
2 Roll out the pastry on a lightly floured surface to a 3 mm/⅛ in thickness and stamp out 6 rounds using a plain 10 cm/4 in cutter.
3 Mix together the currants, mixed peel, butter, 15 g/½ oz of the demerara sugar and the allspice. Divide the mixture between the pastry rounds, dampen the edges and fold them in to enclose the filling, pressing the edges together to seal.
4 Turn the cakes over and flatten slightly with a rolling pin until the fruit just begins to show through the pastry on top. Cut 2 slits in the centre with a sharp knife and place in a circle on the prepared rack.
5 Cook on HIGH for 4–5 minutes, until dry on top. Leave to stand for 5 minutes, then brush with water and sprinkle with the remaining sugar. Transfer to a grill pan and brown the tops under the grill. Makes 6.

## STRAWBERRY AND CUSTARD SLICES

*Puff pastry is a little tricky to cook in the microwave. It rises quickly, but doesn't actually set until the very end of the cooking time and will sink if you open the door before the time is up. The plain pastry looks quite unappealing, but you can transform it into mouthwatering cakes with the addition of strawberry jam and a microwaved custard filling, and pretty icing.*

◆

½ quantity Thick Vanilla Custard (see p. 113)
225 g/8 oz packet puff pastry
4 tbsp strawberry jam
½ quantity Glacé Icing (see p. 114)
few drops of pink food colouring

◆

1 Cover a microwave rack with a double layer of absorbent paper. Make the vanilla custard and leave to cool.
2 Roll out the pastry on a lightly floured surface to a 35 × 40cm/14 × 16 in rectangle. Trim edges to make a neat rectangle and cut in half lengthways. Prick all over with a fork, then cut each piece in 3 crossways to make 6 rectangles.
3 Place 2 pastry rectangles at a time on the prepared rack and cook on HIGH for 3–3½ minutes, until crisp. Transfer to a wire rack to cool. Using a sharp bread knife, trim the edges of the pastry and cut each piece in 3 crossways. Sandwich 3 layers at a time with the jam and custard.
4 Make the glacé icing, put 1 tbsp of the icing in a cup and colour pink, then spoon into a paper piping bag. Spread the remaining icing over the tops of the pastries, then immediately pipe 3 or 4 fine lines of pink icing across the top. Quickly draw a skewer across the piped lines, first in one direction, then in the other to make a feather pattern. Leave to set for 30 minutes. Makes 6.

# Orange And Caraway Castles

*These tangy little cakes are made in the microwave equivalent of dariole moulds – paper cups. I found that the cakes turned out easily from slightly waxed cups, but if yours are made of plain paper line the bases with rounds of baking parchment to stop them sticking.*

◆

75 g/3 oz butter
50 g/2 oz caster sugar
5 tbsp orange marmalade
grated rind of ½ orange
1 tbsp orange juice
2 eggs, beaten
115 g/4 oz self-raising flour, sifted
pinch of salt
½ tsp caraway seeds
15 g/½ oz cornflakes, crushed

◆

1 Grease 8 paper cups and arrange in a circle on a large plate.
2 Put the butter in a mixing bowl and cook on HIGH for 15 seconds to soften. Add the sugar, 2 tbsp of the marmalade, the orange rind and juice, eggs, flour, salt and caraway seeds. Beat together until well blended.
3 Divide the mixture between the cups and cook on HIGH for 3 minutes, or until springy to touch. Leave to stand for 3 minutes, then turn out on to a wire rack to cool.
4 Put the remaining marmalade into a small bowl and cook on HIGH for 30–45 seconds to melt. Sieve, reserving the shreds for decoration. Brush the cakes with marmalade and roll in the cornflakes to coat. Decorate the tops with the orange rind. Makes 8.

# Florentine Slices

*These slices are very simple to make and taste really good. The mixture is very sticky so is sure to be a childrens' favourite; in fact, it's one that a child could easily make on their own – although you should lend a hand when the biscuits are ready to come out of the cooker as the dish gets extremely hot.*

◆

175 g/6 oz plain chocolate
150 g/5 oz sultanas
50 g/2 oz cornflakes, crushed
75 g/3 oz unsalted roasted peanuts
50 g/2 oz glacé cherries, washed, dried and quartered
150 ml/¼ pint condensed milk

◆

1 Grease and base-line a 15 × 23 cm/6 × 9 in cake dish.
2 Break the chocolate into squares and put in a small bowl. Cook on MEDIUM for 4 minutes, then stir to melt. Spread over the base of the prepared dish and leave to cool, then chill until set.
3 Put the sultanas, cornflakes, peanuts, glacé cherries and condensed milk in a bowl and mix well. Spread over the chocolate and smooth with the back of a spoon.
4 Cook on MEDIUM for 10 minutes, leave to cool in the dish, then chill for about 30 minutes, until set. Turn out of the dish on to a board and cut into 15 squares with a sharp knife.

Butterfly cakes, Fresh fruit fondants

## FRESH FRUIT FONDANTS

*Strawberries and mandarin orange segments are used to decorate these cakes, but you could substitute pineapple wedges, apricot halves, raspberries or cherries. Colour the icing to suit.*

◆

115 g/4 oz butter
115 g/4 oz caster sugar
2 eggs, beaten
115 g/4 oz self-raising flour, sifted
2 tbsp milk
few drops of vanilla essence
1 tsp icing sugar
75 ml/3 fl oz double cream, whipped
8 strawberries
7 mandarin orange segments
1 quantity Fondant Icing (see p. 118)
few drops of pink and orange food colouring

◆

1 Grease and base-line a 15 × 23 cm/6 × 9 in cake dish.
2 Put the butter in a mixing bowl and cook on HIGH for 20 seconds to soften. Add the sugar, eggs, flour, milk and vanilla essence. Beat until well blended.
3 Spoon the mixture into the prepared dish and cook on HIGH for 5 minutes, or until a skewer pushed into the centre comes out clean. Leave to stand for 5 minutes, then turn out and cool on a wire rack.
4 Trim the top surface of the cake if it is uneven, then cut the cake into 15 squares. Remove a small piece from the centre of each using an apple corer.
5 Stir the icing sugar and a few drops of vanilla essence into the cream and spoon or pipe a little into the centre of each cake and top with a piece of fresh fruit.
6 Put the fondant icing in a bowl and cook on HIGH for 1½–2½ minutes until melted, then stir in 2 tbsp water. Pour half into a separate bowl and colour pale pink. Colour the other half pale orange.
7 Arrange the cakes, evenly spaced, on a wire rack over a plate and spoon the fondant over the cakes to coat, using the pink icing for the strawberry cakes and orange for the mandarin ones. Leave to set for 30 minutes. Makes 15.

## BUTTERFLY CAKES

*Plastic bun trays are ideal for small cakes, because they are specially designed for microwave cooking. If you don't have one you can use small cups or ramekins to hold the paper cases – arrange them in a circle on a plate.*

◆

50 g/2 oz butter
50 g/2 oz caster sugar
1 egg, beaten
50 g/2 oz self-raising flour, sifted
grated rind of ½ lemon
1 tbsp milk
75 ml/3 fl oz double cream, whipped
drinking chocolate powder for dusting

◆

1 Place 12 paper cake cases in the hollows of 2 bun trays (6 in each).
2 Put the butter in a mixing bowl and cook on HIGH for 15 seconds to soften. Add the sugar, egg, flour, lemon rind and milk and beat until well blended.
3 Divide the mixture between the cake cases and cook (one tray at a time) on HIGH for 1½–2 minutes, until springy to touch. Leave to stand for 3 minutes, then transfer to a wire rack to cool.
4 Cut a small round cone of sponge from the top of each cake. Cut the rounds in half and set aside.
5 Spoon a little of the cream on to each cake and push the halved tops into the cream to look like butterfly wings. Dust with chocolate powder. Makes 12.

## Cherry Bakewell Bars

*Wash the sugary coating from glacé cherries before you use them, otherwise they can become very hot during microwaving and may make the cake overheat and dry out.*

75 g/3 oz plain flour
pinch of salt
130 g/4½ oz butter
75 g/3 oz light soft brown sugar
1 egg, beaten
75 g/3 oz self-raising flour
75 g/3 oz ground almonds
2 tbsp milk
115 g/4 oz glacé cherries, halved, washed and dried
25 g/1 oz flaked almonds, toasted (see p. 120)

1 Grease and base-line a 15 × 23 cm/6 × 9 in cake dish.
2 Sift the plain flour and salt into a mixing bowl and rub in 40 g/1½ oz of the butter until the mixture resembles breadcrumbs. Mix in enough water to make a soft dough, about 1–2 tbsp.
3 Roll out the pastry on a lightly floured surface to fit base of the dish. Press into the base of the dish and prick all over with a fork. Cover with a piece of absorbent paper and add a layer of ceramic baking beans. Cook on HIGH for 4 minutes, remove the paper and beans and cook for a further 1 minute.
4 Put the remaining butter in a mixing bowl and cook on HIGH for 15 seconds to soften. Add the sugar and beat until light and fluffy. Beat in the egg, a little at a time, beating well after each addition.
5 Sift the self-raising flour into the bowl and fold into the mixture with the ground almonds and milk. Scatter over the cherries, then spoon the mixture over the pastry in the dish and spread evenly. Cook on HIGH for 3 minutes, then sprinkle the flaked almonds over the top.
6 Cook on HIGH for a further 2½–3½ minutes, until springy to touch. Leave to stand for 5 minutes, then turn out on to a wire rack to cool. Cut into 12 slices.

## Hazel Nutties

*These tiny little cakes topped with whole toasted hazelnuts are cooked in petit four cases which must be made of paper, not foil. If the cases are very thin, use a double layer for added strength.*

50 g/2 oz butter
25 g/1 oz caster sugar
25 g/1 oz ground hazelnuts
50 g/2 oz plain flour, sifted
1 egg yolk
12 toasted hazelnuts

1 Place 12 double petit four cases in a circle on a large plate.
2 Put the butter in a bowl and cook on HIGH for 15 seconds to soften. Add the sugar and beat until light and fluffy. Stir in the hazelnuts, flour and egg yolk and mix to a soft dough.
3 Divide the mixture into 12 and roll into balls. Place one in each of the double cases and top each with a toasted hazelnut. Cook on HIGH for 2½–3 minutes, until firm to the touch. Leave to stand for 3 minutes, then cool on a wire rack. Makes 12.

## ST CLEMENTS CAKES

*To get the maximum amount of juice from citrus fruits, grate the rind from the whole fruit, then cook each fruit on High for 30 seconds – the warm fruit will produce much more juice when squeezed.*

◆

115 g/4 oz butter
115 g/4 oz caster sugar
2 eggs, beaten
115 g/4 oz self-raising flour, sifted
grated rind and juice of ½ lemon
grated rind and juice of ½ orange
½ quantity Lemon Butter Cream (see p. 112)
½ quantity Orange Butter Cream (see p. 112)

◆

1 Place 10 paper cake cases in the hollows of 2 bun trays (5 in each).
2 Put the butter in a mixing bowl and cook on HIGH for 20 seconds to soften. Add the sugar and beat until light and fluffy. Beat in the eggs, a little at a time, beating well after each addition. Fold in the flour with the lemon and orange rind.
3 Divide the mixture between the cake cases and smooth the surfaces. Cook (one tray at a time) on HIGH for 1½–2 minutes, until springy to the touch. Leave to stand for 5 minutes, then transfer to a wire rack to cool.
4 Make the butter creams and put into separate piping bags each fitted with a 5 mm/¼ in star nozzle. Pipe the icings in alternate lines on top of the cakes to give a stripy effect. Makes 10.

## RASPBERRY SNOWBALLS

*Microwaved sponge is very soft, so you can make ball shaped cakes without rounded dishes. The cakes have flat bases, but once they are dipped in the jam and coconut they mould easily into balls and look very effective.*

◆

50 g/2 oz butter
½ tsp vanilla essence
50 g/2 oz caster sugar
1 egg, beaten
75 g/3 oz self-raising flour, sifted
2 tbsp milk
6 tbsp raspberry jam
50 g/2 oz desiccated coconut

◆

1 Grease 5 hollows in each of 2 bun trays.
2 Put the butter in a mixing bowl and cook on HIGH for 15 seconds to soften. Add the vanilla essence and sugar and beat until light and fluffy. Add the egg, a little at a time, beating well after each addition, then stir in the flour and milk.
3 Divide the mixture between the prepared bun trays and cook (one tray at a time) on HIGH for 1½ minutes, or until springy to touch. Leave to stand for 3 minutes, then transfer to a wire rack to cool.
4 Remove the paper cases and sandwich the cakes in pairs with about half of the jam. Add 2 tbsp water to the remaining jam and cook on HIGH for 30–60 seconds to melt.
5 Dip the sponges in the jam, then roll in the coconut to coat completely. Leave to set for 30 minutes. Makes 5.

Sultana cheesecake squares, Brummy buns page 41

# SULTANA CHEESECAKE SQUARES

*To make sure it sets smoothly, cheesecake needs gentle cooking. Watch the topping for the last 5 minutes of the cooking time and if it begins to boil, switch off the cooker and leave the cake to stand for a few minutes before continuing.*

◆

75 g/3 oz plain flour
40 g/1½ oz butter, diced
100 g/3½ oz caster sugar
3 eggs plus 1 yolk
350 g/12 oz skimmed milk soft cheese
grated rind of 2 oranges
¼ tsp grated nutmeg
75 g/3 oz sultanas
icing sugar, to dust

◆

1 Grease and base-line a 15 × 23 cm/6 × 9 in cake dish.
2 Sift the flour into a mixing bowl and rub in the butter until the mixture resembles fine breadcrumbs. Stir in 40 g/1½ oz sugar and one egg yolk, then mix in enough water to give a firm dough, about 1 tbsp.
3 On a lightly floured surface, roll out the dough to fit the base of the dish. Press into the prepared dish and prick all over. Cover with a sheet of absorbent paper and add a layer of ceramic baking beans. Cook on HIGH for 3 minutes, remove the beans and paper and cook on HIGH for 1 minute.
4 Leave the pastry to stand while preparing the cheesecake mixture; put the cheese in a bowl with the remaining sugar, eggs, orange rind and nutmeg and beat until smooth, then stir in the sultanas.
5 Pour into the dish on top of the pastry and spread evenly. Cook on HIGH for 2 minutes, and DEFROST for 10–12 minutes, until just set in the middle. Leave to cool, then chill for 30 minutes. Turn out and dust with sugar. Cut into 15 squares.

# LEMON DATE SCONE SANDWICH

*These square-cut scones are ideal for packed lunches and picnics. They have a moist texture and tangy flavour that is full of goodness. Dates are suggested here, but they would also be excellent filled with figs and flavoured with orange.*

◆

150 g/5 oz stoned dates, chopped
grated rind and juice of 1 lemon
225 g/8 oz self-raising flour
pinch of salt
50 g/2 oz butter, diced
50 g/2 oz light soft brown sugar
1 egg, beaten
about 4 tbsp milk
caster sugar, to dust

◆

1 Grease and base-line a shallow 25 cm/10 in round cake dish or plate.
2 Put the dates, lemon rind and juice in a small bowl, cover and cook on HIGH for 3 minutes, or until the dates are softened. Beat to a thick paste and leave to cool.
3 Sift the flour and salt into a bowl. Rub in the butter until the mixture resembles fine breadcrumbs, then stir in the brown sugar. Add the egg and enough of the milk to mix to a soft, but not sticky dough.
4 Knead lightly on a floured surface, then cut in half and roll out each piece to a 20 cm/8 in round. Put one into the prepared dish and brush the edge with milk. Spread the date mixture to within 1 cm/½ in of the edge, then cover with the second round.
5 Mark into 12 wedges, then cook on HIGH for 6–7 minutes, until well risen and springy to the touch. Dust with caster sugar and leave to stand for 10 minutes, then break into 12 wedges and serve warm.

# Lemon And Coconut Cakes

*These sound a bit of a fiddle because they are made in 3 layers, but in fact the mixture takes only 12 minutes to cook and I think you will find it well worth the effort. After you have tasted the creamy lemon filling, it is hard to resist a second slice.*

◆

75 g/3 oz butter
75 g/3 oz caster sugar
75 g/3 oz plain flour
25 g/1 oz cornflour
400 ml/14 fl oz condensed milk
2 eggs, separated
grated rind and juice of 1 lemon
50 g/2 oz desiccated coconut
25 g/1 oz flaked coconut, toasted (see p. 120)

◆

1 Grease and base-line a 15 × 23 cm/6 × 9 in cake dish.
2 Put the butter in a mixing bowl and cook on HIGH for 15 seconds to soften. Add 25 g/1 oz of the sugar and beat until light and fluffy. Sift in the flours and add enough water to mix to a firm dough, about 1 tbsp.
3 Knead lightly and press into the base of the prepared dish. Prick all over with a fork and cook on HIGH for 3 minutes, until dry on top.
4 Put the condensed milk, egg yolks, lemon rind and juice into a bowl and cook on HIGH for 3 minutes, whisking 3 or 4 times. Pour into the dish over the pastry, spread evenly and cook on MEDIUM for 3 minutes.
5 Beat the egg whites in a separate bowl until holding soft peaks. Add the remaining sugar, a little at a time, whisking after each addition. Fold in the desiccated coconut and spoon over the lemon filling.
6 Sprinkle the flaked coconut over the top and cook on MEDIUM for a further 2½–3 minutes, until the meringue is just set. Leave to stand for 10 minutes, then turn out on to a wire rack to cool. Cut into 10 bars.

# Apricot Buns

*A hint of ginger gives these little buns a golden colour. They can be eaten plain – warm from the cooker – or cooled and topped with sliced apricots and a shiny glaze.*

◆

115 g/4 oz self-raising flour
pinch of salt
¾ tsp ground ginger
50 g/2 oz butter
50 g/2 oz light soft brown sugar
about 4 tbsp milk
200 g/7 oz canned apricot halves, drained
½ quantity Apricot Jam Glaze (see p. 124)

◆

1 Place 12 paper cake cases in the hollows of 2 bun trays.
2 Sift the flour, salt and ginger into a mixing bowl. Rub in the butter until the mixture resembles fine breadcrumbs, then stir in the sugar. Mix in enough of the milk to give a soft dropping consistency.
3 Weigh out 50 g/2 oz of the apricot halves and chop. Stir into the cake mixture, then divide between the cake cases. Cook (one tray at a time) on HIGH for 1½–2 minutes, until springy to touch. Leave to stand for 3 minutes, then transfer to a wire rack to cool.
4 Thickly slice the remaining apricot halves and arrange 3 or 4 on top of each cake. Make the apricot glaze and brush over the top of each cake, while still warm. Leave to set for 10 minutes. Makes 12.

## Cherry Scones

*These microwaved scones can be made extra soft and light by substituting sour milk or buttermilk for fresh – the additional acid helps the scones rise even more.*

◆

175 g/6 oz self-raising flour
pinch of salt
40 g/1 ½ oz butter, diced
40 g/1 ½ oz caster sugar
40 g/1 ½ oz glacé cherries, washed, dried and chopped
1 egg, beaten
about 3 tbsp milk
plain flour for dusting

◆

1 Grease a baking tray or large plate.
2 Sift the flour and salt into a mixing bowl. Rub in the butter until the mixture resembles fine breadcrumbs, then stir in the sugar and cherries. Add the egg and enough of the milk to mix to a soft, but not sticky dough.
3 Turn out on to a floured surface and knead lightly. Pat out to a 2 cm/¾ in thickness and stamp out 8 rounds using a plain 5 cm/2 in cutter. Dust the tops with flour and arrange in a circle on a baking tray.
4 Cook on HIGH for 4 minutes, or until well risen and firm to the touch. Leave to stand for 5 minutes, then brown under a hot grill. Makes 8.

## Treacle Scones

*Scones are very plain, light cakes. They take their name from the town of Scone in Scotland and would originally have been cooked on a griddle over a peat fire. They work exceptionally well in the modern microwave, but are still best eaten in the traditional way – warm from the cooker, split and spread with butter.*

◆

225 g/8 oz wholewheat self-raising flour
1 tsp baking powder
½ tsp mixed spice
pinch of salt
50 g/2 oz butter, diced
25 g/1 oz light soft brown sugar
50 g/2 oz sultanas
1 tbsp black treacle
about 150 ml/¼ pint milk

◆

1 Grease a baking tray or large plate.
2 Sift the flour, baking powder, spice and salt into a mixing bowl. Rub in the butter until the mixture resembles fine breadcrumbs, then add the sugar, sultanas and treacle. Mix in enough of the milk to make a soft dough.
3 Turn the dough out on to a floured board, knead lightly, then pat out to a 20 cm/8 in round and mark into 8 wedges.
4 Place on the prepared baking tray and cook on HIGH for 5 minutes, or until well risen and springy to touch. Leave to stand for 5 minutes, then break into 8 wedges and serve warm, split and spread with butter. Makes 8.

# STRAWBERRY TARTS

*Rich pastry, rolled thinly, becomes quite crisp during microwaving because it has a high fat and sugar content. However, these ingredients can also make the pastry burn. Watch the cases carefully during the last minute of cooking and remove them if they brown.*

◆

115 g/4 oz plain flour
pinch of salt
50 g/2 oz butter, diced
50 g/2 oz caster sugar
2 egg yolks
few drops of vanilla essence
1 quantity Redcurrant Jelly Glaze (see p. 124)
350 g/12 oz strawberry fromage frais
12 fresh strawberries

◆

1 Sift the flour and salt into a mixing bowl and rub in the butter until the mixture resembles fine breadcrumbs. Add the sugar, egg yolks and vanilla essence and mix to a firm dough.

2 Knead lightly, then roll out on a floured surface to a 3 mm/⅛ in thickness. Stamp out 12 rounds with a plain 10 cm/4 in cutter and use to line the hollows of 2 bun trays. Prick the pastry all over and chill for 10 minutes.

3 Line the pastry cases with baking parchment and fill with ceramic baking beans. Cook (one tray at a time) on HIGH for 2 minutes, remove the paper and beans and cook for a further 30–60 seconds, until the pastry is firm to the touch.

4 Leave to stand for 3 minutes, then turn out on to a wire rack to cool. Make the redcurrant jelly glaze, then divide the fromage frais between the pastry cases. Top each with a strawberry and brush with the glaze. Leave to set for 10 minutes. Makes 12.

From the top clockwise: Cherry and almond baklava page 40, Strawberry tarts, Frangipane flans page 40

## FRANGIPANE FLANS

*Microwaved pastry has a tendency to become bubbly and soft. To get the best results, roll it out thinly and prick all over with a fork. Line with absorbent paper to keep it dry and fill with ceramic beans to keep the shape.*

◆

115 g/4 oz plain flour
50 g/2 oz wholewheat flour
pinch of salt
50 g/2 oz butter
25 g/1 oz caster sugar
1 egg, beaten
1 quantity Frangipane Cream (see p. 112)
425 g/15 oz canned apricot halves, drained
1 quantity Apricot Jam Glaze (see p. 124)
15 g/½ oz flaked almonds, toasted (see p. 120)

◆

1 Sift the flours and salt into a mixing bowl and tip in the bran caught in the sieve. Rub in the butter until the mixture resembles fine breadcrumbs, then add the sugar and egg. Mix together to form a firm dough, adding a little water if necessary.

2 Roll out the dough on a lightly floured surface to a thickness of 3 mm/⅛ in and use to line six 10 cm/4 in fluted flan dishes. Trim the edges neatly and prick all over with a fork. Chill for 10 minutes.

3 Place a piece of absorbent paper in each and fill with ceramic baking beans. Cook 3 at a time on HIGH for 3 minutes, remove the paper and beans and cook for a further 30–60 seconds, until the pastry is firm to the touch.

4 Leave the pastry cases to stand for 3 minutes, then remove from the dishes and leave upside-down on a wire rack to cool.

5 Make the frangipane cream and divide between the pastry cases. Cut the apricot pieces in half and arrange 4 or 5 pieces on top of each flan. Make the glaze and brush over the tops to coat. Sprinkle with the almonds and leave for 10 minutes. Makes 6.

## CHERRY AND ALMOND BAKLAVA

*Thaw the sheets of filo pastry in their wrapping at room temperature for 3 hours, then use at once. Keep unused sheets covered while you work.*

◆

225 g/8 oz unsalted butter
400 g/14 oz packet frozen filo pastry, thawed
175 g/6 oz flaked almonds
225 g/8 oz glacé cherries, washed, dried and chopped
350 g/12 oz caster sugar
450 ml/¾ pint water
1 tbsp lemon juice
2 tbsp rose water

◆

1 Grease and base-line a 20 × 28 cm/8 × 11 in dish.

2 Put the butter in a small bowl and cook on HIGH for 1½–2 minutes to melt. Cut the pastry sheets in half crossways. Layer one third of them in the dish, brushing each one liberally with butter.

3 Mix together the almonds and cherries and spread half of them in an even layer over the pastry. Continue layering the remaining pastry sheets and butter, adding a second layer of almonds and cherries halfway through.

4 Brush the rest of the butter over the top layer of pastry. Cook on HIGH for 10–12 minutes, or until the pastry is crisp and beginning to brown. Leave to stand for 5 minutes.

5 Put the sugar, water, lemon juice and rose water in a large bowl and cook on HIGH for 4 minutes, then stir to dissolve the sugar. Cook on HIGH for a further 6–8 minutes, until thickened and syrupy. Leave the syrup to cool for 5 minutes, then spoon over the baklava and leave in a cool place overnight. Cut into about 32 triangles.

## BRUMMY BUNS

*I'm not sure where the idea for these buns originates (apart from Birmingham that is!). They are made in the same way as Chelsea buns, but using scone dough in place of the usual yeasty mixture. They are cooked in a circle and the buns should fit quite snugly so that they join into a ring as they cook – don't be tempted to use larger dishes than suggested.*

◆

65 g/2½ oz butter, diced
75 g/3 oz sultanas
75 g/3 oz glacé cherries, chopped
½ tsp mixed spice
25 g/1 oz demerara sugar
2 tsp lemon juice
75 g/3 oz chopped toasted hazelnuts
225 g/8 oz self-raising flour
½ tsp baking powder
pinch of salt
50 g/2 oz light soft brown sugar
about 150 ml/¼ pint milk
½ quantity Glacé Icing (see p. 114)

◆

1 Grease and base-line two 20 cm/8 in sandwich cake dishes.
2 Put 15 g/½ oz of the butter in a bowl and cook on HIGH for 30 seconds to melt. Stir in the sultanas, 50 g/2 oz of the glacé cherries, the spice, demerara sugar, lemon juice and 50 g/2 oz of the hazelnuts. Set aside.
3 Sift the flour, baking powder and salt into a mixing bowl and rub in the remaining butter. Add the soft brown sugar and enough of the milk to make a soft dough.
4 Turn out on to a floured surface and knead lightly. Roll out to a 15 × 40 cm/6 × 16 in rectangle. Brush with a little milk, then spread the fruit mixture evenly over the top.
5 Roll up firmly from one long side, then cut across into 12 rounds. Place half of the rounds in a circle in each of the prepared dishes. Cook (one dish at a time) on HIGH for 3 minutes, or until well risen and springy to the touch.
6 Leave to stand for 5 minutes, then turn out on to a wire rack to cool. Make the glacé icing and drizzle over the tops while the bun rings are still warm. Sprinkle immediately with the remaining nuts and cherries, then leave to cool and set for 30 minutes. Break into 12 buns.

## CHOCOLATE AND COCONUT CRUNCH

*This scrumptious cake is simplicity itself – you mix and microwave it in the same dish so there's only one dish to wash up. Make sure you drizzle the condensed milk evenly over the dry ingredients otherwise it will cook unevenly.*

◆

75 g/3 oz butter
115 g/4 oz digestive biscuits, crushed
115 g/4 oz plain chocolate drops
100 g/3½ oz desiccated coconut, toasted (see p. 120)
115 g/4 oz chopped toasted hazelnuts
400 ml/14 fl oz condensed milk

◆

1 Grease and base-line a 15 × 23 cm/6 × 9 in cake dish.
2 Put the butter into the prepared dish and cook on HIGH for 1 minute to melt. Sprinkle the biscuit crumbs, chocolate drops, coconut and hazelnuts into the dish in an even layer.
3 Drizzle the condensed milk over the top and cook on MEDIUM for 10 minutes. Leave to cool in the dish, then chill for about 30 minutes, until set. Cut into 16 rectangles with a sharp knife.

There's no doubt that the bonus of microwaving biscuits is the speed with which they cook. Some of the recipes are so quick that if you have a store cupboard stocked with the right ingredients they can be mixed and cooked by the time the kettle has boiled and the tea infused.

Many different types of biscuits can be microwaved, but most are not as crisp as conventional biscuits, though they still make very good eating. There are simple, speedy stamped-out rounds, such as Ginger Thins and Currant Biscuits; biscuits that need rolling and shaping, like the prettily decorated Spring Garlands and butter cream-filled Glazed Orange Ovals; and others, like the elegant Coffee Catherine Wheels that are more time-consuming to make, but are ideal if you want to impress guests.

Savoury biscuits work very well too – Cheddar Cheese Twists and Curried Cheese Biscuits both become quite crisp on cooling and would make delicious nibbles for parties, with or without a dip.

It's important that you check biscuits during cooking (especially towards the end of the time). They are relatively high in fat and sugar, so are prone to overheating. Remove any that are ready before the others, but remember that once you have reduced the quantity of food in the cooker, the remainder will cook more quickly.

CHAPTER THREE

# BISCUITS

## CHERRY NUT COOKIES

*Watch these cookies carefully during the last minute of cooking as they become very hot in the centre and can burn if cooked too long.*

50 g/2 oz butter
25 g/1 oz caster sugar
1 egg yolk
½ tsp vanilla essence
65 g/2½ oz self-raising flour, sifted
50 g/2 oz chopped mixed nuts, toasted (see p. 120)
8 glacé cherries, halved

1 Line 2 baking trays with pieces of baking parchment.
2 Put the butter in a bowl and cook on HIGH for 15 seconds to soften. Add the sugar and beat until light and fluffy. Add the egg yolk and beat well, then stir in the vanilla essence and flour and mix to a firm dough.
3 Divide the mixture into 16 pieces and roll into balls. Spread the nuts on a plate and roll the balls in the nuts to coat. Arrange 8 balls in a circle on each tray.
4 Wash the cherry halves to remove the sugar syrup, then dry on absorbent paper. Press one into the centre of each ball, flattening the balls slightly.
5 Cook (one tray at a time) on HIGH for 2–2½ minutes, until firm to the touch. Leave to stand for 3 minutes, then transfer to a wire rack to cool. Makes 16.

## COCONUT CIRCLES

*The top layer of these sandwiched biscuits has a small circle stamped out of the centre so you can see the raspberry jam filling. Dust them with icing sugar after sandwiching – the icing sugar coating on the jam soon dissolves to leave the original red colour.*

50 g/2 oz plain flour
50 g/2 oz butter, diced
50 g/2 oz light soft brown sugar
50 g/2 oz desiccated coconut, toasted (see p. 120)
1 egg yolk
2 tbsp raspberry jam
icing sugar, to dust

1 Line 2 baking trays with pieces of baking parchment.
2 Sift the flour into a mixing bowl and rub in the butter until the mixture resembles fine breadcrumbs. Stir in the sugar, coconut and egg yolk and mix to a soft dough.
3 Knead lightly and roll out on a floured surface to a 5 mm/¼ in thickness. Stamp out 16 rounds using a fluted 5 cm/2 in cutter. Cut out the centres from half the circles with an apple corer (do this before you re-roll the dough for the last few biscuits).
4 Arrange 8 biscuits in a circle on each of the trays. Cook (one tray at a time) on HIGH for 2–2½ minutes, until firm to the touch. Leave to stand for 3 minutes, then transfer to a wire rack to cool.
5 Spread the whole biscuits with raspberry jam, top each with a ring biscuit and dust with icing sugar. Makes 8.

## CURRANT BISCUITS

*These simple biscuits are lightly flavoured with orange. When you're only using half an orange for flavouring, grate the rind from the whole orange before you cut it in half to squeeze the juice.*

50 g/2 oz butter
50 g/2 oz light soft brown sugar
115 g/4 oz wholewheat flour, sifted
25 g/1 oz currants
grated rind of 1 orange
juice of ½ orange

1 Line 2 baking trays with pieces of baking parchment.
2 Put the butter in a bowl and cook on HIGH for 15 seconds to soften. Add the sugar and beat until light and fluffy. Stir in the flour, currants and orange rind, then mix in enough of the juice to make a firm dough.
3 Knead lightly and roll out on a floured surface to a 5 mm/¼ in thickness. Stamp out 16 rounds using a fluted 5 cm/2 in cutter.
4 Arrange 8 in a circle on each of the prepared trays and cook (one tray at a time) on HIGH for 2–2½ minutes, until firm to the touch. Leave to stand for 3 minutes, then transfer to a wire rack to cool. Makes 16.

## GINGER THINS

*Roll out these gingery biscuits very thinly and they will become crisp as they cool.*

50 g/2 oz butter
40 g/1½ oz light soft brown sugar
75 g/3 oz plain flour
pinch of salt
¾ tsp ground ginger

1 Line 2 baking trays with pieces of baking parchment.
2 Put the butter in a bowl and cook on HIGH for 15 seconds to soften. Add the sugar and beat until light and fluffy. Sift in the flour, salt and ginger and mix to a soft dough.
3 Roll out the dough on a floured surface to a 3 mm/⅛ in thickness. Stamp out 12 rounds using a plain 5 cm/2 in cutter.
4 Arrange 6 rounds in a circle on each tray. Cook (one tray at a time) on MEDIUM for 4½–5 minutes, until the biscuits are dry on top. Leave to stand for 3 minutes, then transfer to a wire rack to cool. Makes 12.

# HAZELNUT TRIANGLES

*These tiny triangular biscuits, flavoured with toasted hazelnuts and topped with a crunchy layer of demerara sugar, are ideal for serving with ice cream.*

◆

75 g/3 oz plain flour
pinch of salt
40 g/1½ oz butter, diced
25 g/1 oz caster sugar
50 g/2 oz shelled hazelnuts, coarsely ground and toasted (see p. 120)
1 tbsp demerara sugar

◆

**1** Line 2 baking trays with pieces of baking parchment.
**2** Sift the flour and salt into a mixing bowl. Rub in the butter until the mixture resembles fine breadcrumbs. Stir in the caster sugar, hazelnuts and enough water to make a soft dough, about 1 tbsp.
**3** Knead lightly and roll out on a floured surface to a 3 mm/⅛ in thickness. Cut into 12 squares, then mark each of the squares into 2 triangles.
**4** Arrange 6 squares in a circle on each baking tray and cook (one tray at a time) on HIGH for 1½–2 minutes, until firm to the touch. Brush with water and sprinkle with demerara sugar, then cook for a further 30 seconds.
**5** Leave to stand for 3 minutes, then transfer to a wire rack to cool. Carefully break the squares along the marked lines to make 24 triangles.

Large plate clockwise from the top: Honey lemon biscuits page 57, Hazelnut triangles, Coconut circles page 44. Small plate: Jumbles page 57

## GINGER COOKIES

*Coloured ingredients like treacle and brown sugar improve the appearance and enhance the flavour of microwaved biscuits. However, they also make the biscuits cook very quickly, so check carefully towards the end of cooking and remove any biscuits that are ready; remember that those that are left will cook even faster.*

◆

115 g/4 oz butter
1 tbsp black treacle
1 tbsp milk
175 g/6 oz self-raising flour
1 tsp ground ginger
¼ tsp bicarbonate of soda
75 g/3 oz light soft brown sugar

◆

1 Line 3 baking trays with pieces of baking parchment.
2 Put the butter and treacle in a mixing bowl and cook on HIGH for 1 minute to melt. Leave to cool. Stir in the milk, then sift in the flour, ginger and bicarbonate of soda. Add the sugar and mix to a firm dough.
3 Divide the mixture into 18 and roll into balls. Arrange 6 in a circle on each of the baking trays and cook (one tray at a time) on MEDIUM for 3–4 minutes, until dry on top. Leave to stand for 3 minutes, then cool on a wire rack. Makes 18.

## CHOCOLATE AND WALNUT COOKIES

*These cookies are lightly flavoured with cocoa and walnuts. Don't chop the walnuts too finely, if they are coarsely chopped they give the cookies a crunchy, rocky texture.*

◆

25 g/1 oz butter
40 g/1 ½ oz light soft brown sugar
2 tbsp golden syrup
1 egg, beaten
few drops of vanilla essence
65 g/2½ oz plain flour
1 tbsp cocoa powder
¼ tsp baking powder
pinch of salt
115 g/4 oz shelled walnuts, chopped

◆

1 Line 2 baking trays with pieces of baking parchment.
2 Put the butter, sugar and syrup in a bowl and cook on HIGH for 1½ minutes. Stir to melt the sugar and leave to cool slightly. Beat in the egg and vanilla essence.
3 Sift in the flour, cocoa, baking powder and salt and mix to a soft dough. Stir in the walnuts. Spoon 5 mounds of the mixture in a circle on each of the prepared trays.
4 Cook (one tray at a time) on MEDIUM for 3–4 minutes, until the cookies are almost dry on top. Leave to stand for 3 minutes, then cool on a wire rack. Makes 10.

## SPRING GARLANDS

*It's difficult to make biscuits really crisp in the microwave because they tend to get too hot in the middle. However, because these garlands are circular they can be cooked until just beginning to brown and they will become crisp as they cool.*

◆

50 g/2 oz butter
75 g/3 oz light soft brown sugar
175 g/6 oz plain flour
pinch of salt
1 tsp milk
½ tsp vanilla essence
crystallized violets, rose petals and mimosa balls, to decorate

◆

1 Line 2 baking trays with pieces of baking parchment.
2 Put the butter in a bowl and cook on HIGH for 15 seconds to soften. Add the sugar and beat until light and fluffy.
3 Sift the flour and salt into the bowl, add the milk and vanilla essence and mix to a firm dough.
4 Knead lightly and divide into 12 pieces. Roll out each piece on a floured board to a thin 30 cm/12 in long sausage. Fold each one in half and carefully twist to form a rope, then press the ends together to make circular garlands.
5 Arrange 6 garlands in a circle on each baking tray and decorate with small pieces of crystallized flowers. Cook (one tray at a time) on MEDIUM for 4½–5 minutes, until dry on top. Leave to stand for 3 minutes, then cool on a wire rack. Makes 12.

## COFFEE CATHERINE WHEELS

*These flavoured biscuits are so easy to make, yet look very effective. The 2 coloured doughs – one vanilla and one coffee – are curled into a tight roll and chilled before slicing into thin biscuits which have a neat spiral design.*

◆

50 g/2 oz butter
50 g/2 oz caster sugar
1 egg yolk
few drops of vanilla essence
115 g/4 oz plain flour, sifted
1 tsp instant coffee powder

◆

1 Line 2 baking trays with pieces of baking parchment.
2 Put the butter in a bowl and cook on HIGH for 15 seconds to soften. Add the sugar and beat until light and fluffy. Beat in the egg yolk and vanilla essence, then add the flour and mix to a soft dough.
**3.** Divide the dough in half and work the coffee into one half. Roll out each piece on a floured surface to a 15 × 20 cm/6 × 8 in rectangle. Place the plain piece on top of the coffee piece and roll them up together from a short end.
4 Wrap the roll in clingfilm and chill for 1 hour. Unwrap and slice into 12 rounds with a large sharp knife. Arrange 6 in a circle on each of the prepared trays. Cook (one tray at a time) on HIGH for 2–2½ minutes, until firm to the touch.
5 Leave to stand for 3 minutes, then transfer to a wire rack to cool. Makes 12.

From the top: Chocolate chocolate cookies, Glazed orange ovals, Spring garlands page 49, Coffee catherine wheels page 49

## Chocolate Chocolate Cookies

*The most chocolatey of cookies – eat them either warm while the chocolate drops are still melted and deliciously gooey, or leave them to cool and add a coating of chocolate to the bases.*

◆

50 g/2 oz butter
50 g/2 oz caster sugar
1 egg, beaten
115 g/4 oz wholewheat self-raising flour
2 tbsp cocoa powder
115 g/4 oz plain chocolate drops
50 g/2 oz plain chocolate

◆

1 Line 2 baking trays with pieces of baking parchment.
2 Put the butter in a mixing bowl and cook on HIGH for 15 seconds. Add the sugar, beat until light and fluffy, then beat in the egg.
3 Sift in the flour and cocoa powder, mix well and stir in the chocolate drops. Spoon 7 mounds of the mixture in a circle on each of the prepared trays.
4 Cook (one tray at a time) on MEDIUM for 3–4 minutes, until the cookies are almost dry on top. Leave to cool on the trays.
5 Break the chocolate into a small bowl and cook on MEDIUM for 3–4 minutes to melt. Spread a little on the bases of the cookies with a serrated-edged scraper and mark into wavy lines. Leave chocolate side up on a wire rack to set. Makes 14.

## Glazed Orange Ovals

*To give these tangy biscuits a professional finish, use a soft pastry brush to ice the tops before you sandwich them. Don't make the icing too thick and brush it in an even layer right to the edge, then leave to set.*

◆

115 g/4 oz butter
50 g/2 oz caster sugar
grated rind of 1½ oranges
175 g/6 oz plain flour, sifted
½ quantity Orange Glacé Icing (see p. 114)
½ quantity Orange Butter Cream (see p. 112)

◆

1 Line 2 baking trays with pieces of baking parchment.
2 Put the butter in a bowl and cook on HIGH for 20 seconds to soften. Beat in the sugar until light and fluffy, then add the orange rind from 1 orange and flour and mix to a firm dough.
3 Knead lightly, divide into 16 and roll into ovals with your hands. Press them flat and arrange 8 in a circle on each tray.
4 Cook (one tray at a time) on HIGH for 2–2½ minutes, until firm to the touch. Leave to stand for 3 minutes.
5 Make the glacé icing, brush over the tops of half the biscuits while they are still warm and sprinkle with the remaining grated orange rind. Transfer to a wire rack to cool and set.
6 Make the butter cream and use to sandwich the biscuits in pairs. Makes 8.

## PECAN NUT BISCUITS

◆

40 g/1½ oz butter
2 tbsp light soft brown sugar
65 g/2½ oz wholewheat flour, sifted
50 g/2 oz pecan nuts, finely chopped
caster sugar, to dust

◆

1 Line 2 baking trays with pieces of baking parchment.
2 Put the butter in a bowl and cook on HIGH for 15 seconds to soften. Add the brown sugar, flour, nuts and enough water to mix to a firm dough, about 1 tbsp.
3 Knead lightly, then roll out on a floured surface to a 20 cm/8 in square and cut into 24 fingers. Arrange 12 in a circle on each of the baking trays.
4 Cook (one tray at a time) on HIGH for 2½–3 minutes, until dry on top. Dust with caster sugar and leave to stand for 3 minutes. Transfer to a wire rack to cool. Makes 24.

## GINGER SHORTCAKES

◆

150 g/5 oz plain flour
pinch of salt
1 tsp ground ginger
115 g/4 oz butter, diced
50 g/2 oz light soft brown sugar
½ quantity Ginger Glacé Icing (see p. 114)

◆

1 Line 3 baking trays with pieces of baking parchment.
2 Sift the flour, salt and ginger into a mixing bowl and work in the butter and sugar until the mixture forms a soft dough.
3 Knead lightly, then roll out on a floured surface to a 5 mm/¼ in thickness. Cut out 9 rounds using a plain 7.5 cm/3 in cutter, then cut the rounds in half.
4 Arrange 6 semi-circles in a circle on each tray and prick all over. Cook (one tray at a time) on HIGH for 2–2½ minutes, until firm to the touch. Leave to stand for 3 minutes, then transfer to a wire rack to cool.
5 Make the glacé icing and brush over the tops of the biscuits while they are still warm, then leave to cool and set on the wire racks. Makes 18.

## SCOTTISH OATCAKES

*Oatcakes are traditionally cut in wedges (known as 'farles'). If the pointed ends are still moist at the end of the cooking time, turn the points to the outside of the dish and cook for an extra minute.*

◆

15 g/½ oz white cooking fat
225 g/8 oz fine oatmeal
¼ tsp salt
¼ tsp bicarbonate of soda

◆

1 Place a double layer of absorbent paper on 2 microwave racks.
2 Put the fat and 150 ml (¼ pint) water in a jug and cook on HIGH for 1½ minutes. Put 115 g/4 oz of the oatmeal, the salt and bicarbonate of soda in a mixing bowl. Add enough of the water and fat to mix to a firm dough, then divide in half.
3 Sprinkle the work surface with a little oatmeal. Knead each piece of the dough lightly and roll out to a 20 cm/8 in round. Dust the tops with oatmeal and cut the rounds into 8 wedges.
4 Place a re-shaped round on each of the prepared racks and cook (one at a time) on HIGH for 4–5 minutes, until dry and beginning to curl. Leave to stand for 3 minutes on the microwave racks, then cool on a wire rack. Makes 16.

# Coconut And Cherry Chewies

*These rocky little biscuits are ideal for a child's first adventure into microwave cooking – they are quick and easy to mix and shape, and they taste delicious.*

◆

115 g/4 oz desiccated coconut
50 g/2 oz cornflakes, crushed
115 g/4 oz glacé cherries, washed, dried and quartered
4 egg whites
115 g/4 oz caster sugar

◆

1 Place 8 paper cases in a circle on each of 2 baking trays.
2 Put the coconut, cornflakes and cherries in a mixing bowl and mix together.
3 In a separate bowl, whisk the egg whites until holding soft peaks, then fold in the sugar. Fold into the coconut mixture until well mixed.
4 Divide the mixture between the cake cases, leaving them rough on top. Cook (one tray at a time) on HIGH for 2–3 minutes, until firm to the touch.
5 Leave to stand for 3 minutes, then transfer to a wire rack to cool. Makes 16.

# Coconut Bars

*Some plastic microwave dishes became quite flexible at high temperatures. If you are using a plastic microwave dish, support it on a baking tray to prevent it twisting when you lift it out of the microwave.*

◆

75 g/3 oz digestive biscuits, crushed
115 g/4 oz butter
115 g/4 oz light soft brown sugar
25 g/1 oz flaked almonds
25 g/1 oz desiccated coconut
115 g/4 oz milk chocolate drops

◆

1 Grease and base-line a 15 × 23 cm/6 × 9 in cake dish.
2 Spread the crumbs over the base of the dish and press down well with the back of a spoon. Put the butter and sugar in a bowl and cook on HIGH for 3 minutes, stirring once. Pour evenly over the biscuits.
3 Mix together the nuts and coconut and sprinkle in an even layer over the top. Cook on HIGH for 2–2 ½ minutes, or until the mixture is bubbling all over.
4 Leave to stand for 3 minutes, then scatter the chocolate drops evenly over the surface. Leave for 2–3 minutes to melt, then spread evenly.
5 Leave to cool in the dish, then chill for 30 minutes before turning out on to a board. Cut into 18 bars.

## Curried Cheese Biscuits

*These crisp little biscuits can be served with soup instead of croûtons.*

◆

40 g/1 ½ oz butter
75 g/3 oz self-raising flour
½ tsp curry powder
pinch each of salt and cayenne pepper
40 g/1 ½ oz Cheddar cheese, finely grated
about 2 tbsp milk
a little rock salt

◆

1 Line 3 baking trays with pieces of baking parchment.
2 Put the butter in a bowl and cook on HIGH for 15 seconds to soften. Sift in the flour, curry powder, salt and cayenne pepper, then add the cheese and enough milk to mix to a soft dough.
3 Knead lightly and roll out on a floured surface to a 5 mm/¼ in thickness. Stamp out 24 rounds with a plain 4 cm/1½ in cutter. Arrange 8 in a circle on each of the prepared baking trays.
4 Cook (one tray at a time) on HIGH for 2–2½ minutes, until dry on top. Leave to stand for 3 minutes, then cool on a wire rack. Sprinkle with a little rock salt. Makes 24.

## Cheddar Cheese Twists

*Rather than arranging the cheese twists like the spokes of a wheel, place them around the edge of the dish (in two rows if necessary). This way they will cook evenly and become crisp all over.*

◆

115 g/4 oz plain flour
¼ tsp salt
pinch of cayenne pepper
50 g/2 oz butter
50 g/2 oz Cheddar cheese, finely grated
1 egg yolk
25 g/1 oz ready salted crisps, crushed

◆

1 Line 3 baking trays with pieces of baking parchment.
2 Sift the flour, salt and cayenne pepper into a mixing bowl. Rub in the butter until the mixture resembles fine breadcrumbs. Stir in the cheese, egg yolk and enough water to mix to a firm dough, about 2 tsp.
3 Knead lightly and roll out on a floured surface to a 5 mm/¼ in thickness. Cut into thirty-six 5 mm/¼ in sticks. Hold the ends of the sticks and twist them in opposite directions.
4 Spread out the crisps on a plate. Keeping the sticks twisted, roll them in the crisps until coated. Arrange 12 in a circle on each of the prepared baking trays.
5 Cook (one tray at a time) on HIGH for 2–2½ minutes, until firm to the touch. Leave to stand for 3 minutes, then transfer to a wire rack to cool. Makes 36.

From the top: Curried cheese biscuits, Peanut butter cookies page 56, Cheddar cheese twists

## PEANUT BUTTER COOKIES

*You'll find these melt-in-the-mouth cookies very hard to resist. They spread out quite a lot during cooking so use large baking trays, and arrange them as far apart as possible to stop them all joining together.*

◆

50 g/2 oz butter
50 g/2 oz peanut butter
grated rind of ½ orange
115 g/4 oz light soft brown sugar
1 egg yolk
115 g/4 oz self-raising flour, sifted
40 g/1½ oz unsalted peanuts, coarsely chopped

◆

1 Line 3 baking trays with pieces of baking parchment.

2 Put the butter in a bowl and cook on HIGH for 15 seconds to soften. Add the peanut butter, orange rind and sugar and beat until light and fluffy. Beat in the egg yolk, then add the flour and peanuts and mix to a soft dough.

3 Divide the dough into 18 pieces and roll into balls. Arrange 6 in a circle on each of the prepared trays and slightly flatten each one with a fork.

4 Cook (one tray at a time) on HIGH for 2–2½ minutes, until firm to the touch. Leave to stand for 3 minutes, then transfer to a wire rack to cool. Makes 18.

## CHEESY DIGESTIVES

*For a good strong flavour choose a mature Cheddar for these biscuits – they are a tasty way of using up any hard or slightly stale pieces of cheese you might have in your refrigerator.*

◆

75 g/3 oz wholewheat flour
pinch of salt
2 tbsp fine oatmeal
40 g/1½ oz white cooking fat
25 g/1 oz Cheddar cheese, finely grated
2 tsp light soft brown sugar
1 egg, beaten

1 Line 2 baking trays with pieces of baking parchment.

2 Sift the flour and salt into a mixing bowl, tipping in any bran caught in the sieve. Stir in the oatmeal, then rub in the fat until the mixture resembles breadcrumbs. Stir in the cheese and sugar and enough of the egg to make a firm dough.

3 Knead lightly and roll out on a floured surface to a 3 mm/⅛ in thickness. Stamp out 12 rounds using a plain 7 cm/2¾ in cutter. Prick the biscuits with a fork.

4 Arrange 6 in a circle on each of the prepared baking trays. Cook (one tray at a time) on HIGH for 2½–3 minutes, until dry on top. Leave to stand for 3 minutes, then cool on a wire rack. Makes 12.

## JUMBLES

*These delightful 'S' shaped almond biscuits look and taste just the same as when they are baked conventionally, but take just a fraction of the time to cook by microwave.*

◆

50 g/2 oz butter
50 g/2 oz light soft brown sugar
1 egg yolk
few drops of almond essence
75 g/3 oz plain flour, sifted
50 g/2 oz ground almonds
icing sugar, to dust

◆

1 Line 2 baking trays with pieces of baking parchment.
2 Put the butter in a bowl and cook on HIGH for 20 seconds to soften. Add the sugar and beat until light and fluffy. Beat in the egg yolk and almond essence, then stir in the flour and almonds and mix to a firm dough.
3 Knead lightly, then roll out on a floured surface to a sausage shape about 1 cm/½ in in diameter. Cut into 10 cm/4 in lengths and form into 'S' shapes.
4 Place 8 in a circle on each baking tray and cook (one tray at a time) on HIGH for 2½–3½ minutes, or until firm to the touch. Leave to stand for 3 minutes.
5 Carefully transfer to a wire rack, using a palette knife, and leave to cool, then dust with icing sugar. Makes 16.

## HONEY LEMON BISCUITS

*Plain microwaved biscuits need a little help sometimes. These have spices added to the mixture to give them a golden colour, then they are dipped in a lemony, honey icing and topped with pale green pistachio nuts. Make sure that the pistachios you buy are unsalted, or substitute toasted chopped almonds or hazelnuts, if you wish.*

◆

25 g/1 oz butter
3 tbsp honey
115 g/4 oz wholewheat self-raising flour, sifted
¼ tsp ground cinnamon
¼ tsp ground ginger
¼ quantity Honey and Lemon Glacé Icing (see p. 114)
25 g/1 oz shelled pistachio nuts, chopped

◆

1 Line 2 baking trays with pieces of baking parchment.
2 Put the butter in a mixing bowl and cook on HIGH for 10 seconds to soften. Add the honey, flour and spices and mix to a firm dough.
3 Roll out between 2 sheets of clingfilm to a 3 mm/⅛ in thickness. Stamp out 16 rounds using a plain 5 cm/2 in cutter. Arrange 8 in a circle on each tray and cook (one tray at a time) on HIGH for 1½ minutes, or until firm to the touch.
4 Leave to stand for 3 minutes. Make the glacé icing and spread the nuts on a plate. While the biscuits are still warm, dip the tops into the icing, then into the nuts. Leave on a wire rack to cool. Makes 16.

These large, richly layered cakes are quite scrumptious–they are the kind of cakes that you eat with a fork and are intended as desserts for dinner parties, but don't let that stop you making one for a family tea. There's something here to tempt everyone, as long as you forget about calorie counting – rich chocolate cakes, featherlight sponges sandwiched with wonderful creamy fillings, crisp rounds of nutty shortcake and many more.

Although these cakes are quite time consuming to
Although these cakes are quite time consuming to
make, some can be prepared in advance. For instance, butter cream-filled cakes like the Brandy and Walnut Cake keep well and so can be made a day in advance, and Toffee Nut Roll can be made weeks ahead and frozen. The others are best made on the day of the party.

Make sure that sponge layers aren't allowed to dry out before assembling the cake. Keep them covered with a clean tea towel while cooling, then wrap tightly in foil until you are ready to fill, ice or frost. Assemble cream-filled sponge cakes about 2 or 3 hours before the party, place the finished cake in a plastic container and keep in a cool place until ready to serve.

To keep the pastry or shortcake layers crisp, gâteaux like Creamy Strawberry Shortcake and Mandarin Sparkle should not be assembled more than 30 minutes before serving.

CHAPTER FOUR

# PARTY GÂTEAUX

## CHOCOLATE ROULADE

*When this roulade is made conventionally it has a tendency to crack, but when it's microwaved the crust stays soft so it rolls up very easily.*

◆

115 g/4 oz plain chocolate
4 eggs, separated
115 g/4 oz caster sugar
icing sugar, to dust
300 ml/½ pint double cream, whipped

◆

1 Line a shallow 25 cm/10 in square dish with baking parchment (or make a double case with baking parchment).
2 Break the chocolate into a bowl, add 3 tbsp water and cook on MEDIUM for 3–4 minutes to melt, stirring once. Leave to cool.
3 Whisk the yolks until light and fluffy, then gradually whisk in the sugar. In a separate bowl, whisk the egg whites until holding soft peaks.
4 Stir the chocolate into the yolks, then fold in the whites. Pour into the prepared dish and tip the dish to make the mixture run into the corners.
5 Cook on HIGH for 7 minutes, or until firm to the touch but still slightly moist on top, rotating the dish a quarter turn every 2 minutes. Leave to stand for 5 minutes.
6 Dust a sheet of baking parchment thickly with icing sugar, then carefully turn the cake out on to the paper. Spread with the cream and roll up from a long side. Cut into 6 thick slices.

## RASPBERRY GRIESTORTE

*Griestorte, roughly translates as semolina flan, but that doesn't do justice to this cake. The semolina gives it a short, slightly crunchy texture and the cake keeps rather better than one made with flour.*

◆

3 eggs, separated
50 g/2 oz light soft brown sugar
grated rind and juice of ½ lemon
50 g/2 oz wholewheat semolina
200 ml/7 fl oz double cream, whipped
115 g/4 oz fresh raspberries
icing sugar, to dust

◆

1 Base-line two 18 cm/7 in round dishes with baking parchment.
2 Put the yolks and sugar in the bowl of an electric mixer and whisk until pale and mousse-like, and the mixture will hold a trail for 10 seconds.
3 Fold in the lemon rind and juice and the semolina. Whisk the egg whites in a separate bowl with clean beaters until holding soft peaks, then fold into the yolk mixture.
4 Divide the mixture between the dishes and spread evenly. Cook (one dish at a time) on HIGH for 1½–2 minutes, until springy to the touch. Leave to stand for 5 minutes, then turn out on to a wire rack to cool.
5 Sandwich together with the cream and raspberries and dust the top with icing sugar. Cut into 6 wedges.

## FRANGIPANE CAKE

*Sprinkling the top of this cake with toasted almonds gives it a baked look – add the almonds after the top has begun to set otherwise they will sink under the surface.*

◆

4 eggs, separated
115 g/4 oz light soft brown sugar
grated rind and juice of ½ lemon
1 tbsp hot water
40 g/1½ oz ground rice
115 g/4 oz ground almonds
115 g/4 oz flaked almonds, toasted (see p. 120)
1 quantity Frangipane Cream (see p. 112)

◆

1 Base-line a deep 20 cm/8 in round dish with baking parchment.
2 Put the yolks, sugar, lemon rind and juice and hot water in the bowl of an electric mixer and whisk until mousse-like, and the mixture will hold a trail for 10 seconds. Fold in the ground rice and ground almonds.
3 Whisk the egg whites in a separate bowl with clean beaters until holding soft peaks and fold into the yolk mixture.
4 Pour into the prepared dish and cook on HIGH for 3 minutes. Sprinkle with the flaked almonds and cook on HIGH for a further 2 minutes, or until springy to the touch.
5 Leave to stand for 5 minutes, then turn out on to a wire rack to cool. Make the frangipane cream while the cake cools, then split the cake horizontally and sandwich together with the frangipane cream. Cut into 8 wedges.

## COFFEE CAKE WITH FRESH FRUIT

*Microwaved sponges can be moistened by sprinkling with a flavoured liquid after cooking – in this case sugar syrup mixed with coffee liqueur. Mexican Kahlua has a strong flavour, but Tia Maria or coffee brandy would be fine.*

◆

4 eggs
115 g/4 oz caster sugar
115 g/4 oz plain flour
1 tsp baking powder
1 quantity Coffee Butter Cream (see p. 112)
2 quantities Sugar Syrup (see p. 120)
4 tbsp coffee liqueur
1 quantity Coffee Glacé Icing (see p. 114)
225–350 g/8–12 oz mixed fresh fruits, sliced

◆

1 Base-line 2 deep 23 cm/9 in ring dishes with baking parchment.
2 Put the eggs and sugar in the bowl of an electric mixer and whisk until pale and mousse-like, and the mixture will hold a trail for 10 seconds.
3 Sift together the flour and baking powder 2 or 3 times, then fold into the egg mixture. Divide the mixture between the dishes and spread evenly.
4 Cook (one dish at a time) on HIGH for 2–2½ minutes, until springy to the touch. Leave to stand for 5 minutes, then turn out on to a wire rack to cool. Make the butter cream.
5 Split the cakes in half horizontally. Mix half the syrup with the coffee liqueur and sprinkle over the cakes. Sandwich together with the butter cream, place on a wire rack over a large plate.
6 Make the glacé icing and spoon over the cake to coat completely. Leave to set for 30 minutes. Mix the remaining syrup with the fruit and pile into the centre of the cake. Serves 10–12.

# CHOCOLATE ORANGE GÂTEAU

*Whisked sponges are difficult to slice very thinly, but because the microwave cooks so quickly you can easily divide the mixture into 6 and cook the layers separately. Don't overcook them or they will be quite crisp instead of spongy.*

◆

4 eggs
175 g/6 oz caster sugar
150 g/5 oz plain flour
pinch salt
grated rind of 1 orange
1 quantity Orange Sugar Syrup (see p. 120)
1 quantity Plain Chocolate Ganache (see p. 113)
75 ml/3 fl oz double cream, whipped
1 tsp drinking chocolate powder, to dust
2 oranges, peeled and segmented

◆

1 Mark a 20 cm/8 in diameter circle on each of 6 sheets of baking parchment.
2 Put the eggs and sugar in the bowl of an electric mixer and whisk until pale and mousse-like, and the mixture will hold a trail for 10 seconds.
3 Sift together the flour and salt 2 or 3 times, then fold into the yolk mixture with the orange rind. Divide the mixture between the prepared sheets and spread out to fill the marked circles.
4 Cook (one at a time) on HIGH for 1½–2 minutes, or until springy to touch. Leave to stand for 2 minutes, then trim each to a neat round with a sharp knife. Peel off the paper and transfer to wire racks to cool.
5 Spoon the syrup equally over the cakes. Make the chocolate ganache, use half to sandwich the rounds together and spread the rest over the top and sides. Pipe 8 whirls of cream on top of the cake and dust with the chocolate powder. Decorate with the orange segments. Cut into 8 wedges.

# COCOA FUDGE CAKE

*Two cocoa-flavoured sponges and a rich frosting that both fills and coats make this one of the most chocolatey of chocolate cakes. Leave the frosting in rough swirls, and to make it look really special (if you've the time and the patience) decorate the top with long chocolate curls known as caraque.*

◆

2 tbsp cocoa powder, sifted
2 tbsp hot water
115 g/4 oz butter
115 g/4 oz light soft brown sugar
2 eggs, beaten
115 g/4 oz self-raising flour, sifted
1 quantity Chocolate Fudge Frosting (see p. 116)
1 quantity Chocolate Caraque (see p. 121)

◆

1 Grease and base-line 2 deep 18 cm/7 in round dishes.
2 Put the cocoa powder in a small bowl, add the water and mix to a smooth paste.
3 Put the butter in a mixing bowl and cook on HIGH for 20 seconds to soften. Add the sugar and cocoa mixture and beat until light and fluffy. Add the eggs a little at a time, beating well after each addition.
4 Fold in the flour and divide the mixture between the prepared dishes. Cook (one at a time) on HIGH for 3 minutes, or until springy to the touch and just shrinking from the sides of the dish.
5 Leave to stand for 5 minutes, then turn out on to a wire rack to cool. Prepare the frosting and use one-third to sandwich the cakes together. Spread the remainder over the top and sides.
6 Make the caraque and arrange it on top of the cake to decorate. Cut into 6 wedges to serve.

From the top: Chocolate orange gâteau, Cocoa fudge cake

## GÂTEAU BIGARREAU

*This is a classic French gâteau that works beautifully in the microwave. The fact that it doesn't brown makes no difference to the appearance, as the sides are coated in fresh cream and crushed praline, and the top covered in a layer of fresh red cherries. When fresh cherries are out of season, use well-drained canned cherries or substitute halved grapes or plums.*

◆

3 eggs
75 g/3 oz caster sugar
75 g/3 oz plain flour
1 tsp baking powder
1 quantity Praline, crushed (see p. 120)
150 ml/¼ pint double cream, whipped
1 quantity Cherry Jam Glaze (see p. 124)
225–350 g/8–12 oz fresh red cherries, stoned

◆

1 Grease and base-line a deep 20 cm/8 in round dish.
2 Put the eggs and sugar in the bowl of an electric mixer and whisk until pale and mousse-like, and the mixture will hold a trail for 10 seconds.
3 Sift the flour and baking powder 2 or 3 times, then fold into the mixture. Pour into the prepared dish and spread evenly. Cook on HIGH for 3–5 minutes, until springy to the touch. Leave to stand for 5 minutes, then turn out on to a wire rack to cool.
4 Make the praline and fold half into the cream. Split the cake horizontally and sandwich together with three-quarters of the praline cream. Spread the rest round the sides and press the remaining praline over the cream.
5 Make the cherry glaze. Arrange the cherries on top of the cake and brush with the glaze. Leave to set for 30 minutes. Serves 8–10.

## PINEAPPLE AND PISTACHIO GÂTEAU

*The delightful, pale green colour of pistachio nuts shows up best when they are chopped. They are expensive, but for a special occasion are worth every penny. There's no reason why you shouldn't substitute other nuts, but first toast them until golden.*

◆

4 eggs
115 g/4 oz caster sugar
115 g/4 oz plain flour
1 tsp baking powder
225 g/8 oz can pineapple pieces
2 tbsp kirsch
75 g/3 oz shelled pistachio nuts, chopped

◆

1 Grease and base-line 3 deep 15 × 23 cm/6 × 9 in dishes.
2 Put the eggs and sugar in the bowl of an electric mixer and whisk until pale and mousse-like, and the mixture will hold a trail for 10 seconds.
3 Sift the flour and baking powder 2 or 3 times, then fold into the egg mixture. Divide between the prepared dishes and spread evenly. Cook (one at a time) on HIGH for 2 minutes, or until springy to the touch. Leave to stand for 3 minutes, then turn out on to a wire rack to cool.
4 Drain the pineapple and reserve. Mix 6 tbsp of the syrup, or juice, with the kirsch and spoon over the cakes.
5 Chop half of the pineapple, drain and fold into the cream. Use half to sandwich the cakes together and spread the rest over the sides and top. Press the pistachios over the sides and decorate the top with the remaining pineapple pieces. Cut in half lengthways, then crossways into 12 thick slices.

# COFFEE AND CARAMEL GÂTEAU

*Caramel frosting is very sweet, but goes well with the strong flavour of this coffee sponge. Spread the frosting while it is still quite soft, then pipe the rosettes once it starts to firm up. It is decorated with squiggly shapes of caramel which will appeal to both adults and children alike.*

◆

4 eggs
115 g/4 oz caster sugar
1 tbsp instant coffee powder
1 tbsp hot water
115 g/4 oz self-raising flour
12 Caramel Shapes (see p. 122)
2 quantities Caramel Frosting (see p. 116)

◆

1 Grease and base-line two 18 cm/7 in square dishes.
2 Put the eggs and sugar in the bowl of an electric mixer and whisk until pale and mousse-like, and the mixture will hold a trail for 10 seconds. Dissolve the coffee in the hot water and stir into the mixture.
3 Sift the flour 2 or 3 times and fold into the mixture. Divide between the prepared dishes and spread evenly. Cook (one at a time) on HIGH for 3 minutes, or until springy to the touch. Leave to stand for 5 minutes, then turn out on to a wire rack to cool.
4 Make the Caramel Shapes and leave to harden. Make the frosting and use one-third to sandwich the cakes together. Reserve 6 tbsp of the remaining frosting for piping and spread the rest over the top and sides of the cake.
5 Put the reserved frosting in a piping bag fitted with a star nozzle and pipe small stars in 4 or 5 diagonal rows on top. Decorate with the Caramel Shapes. Cut into 12 squares.

# TROPICAL LAYER CAKE

*Toasted coconut makes the sponge very moist and gives it a lovely speckled appearance. The cake is filled and topped with cream and sliced fruits. This recipe uses banana, mango and star fruit, but the cake would be just as good with other fruits. The fruits don't even have to be tropical – just tangy and colourful.*

◆

50 g/2 oz butter
115 g/4 oz caster sugar
2 eggs, beaten
75 g/3 oz desiccated coconut, toasted (see p. 120)
350 g/12 oz self-raising flour, sifted
150 ml/¼ pint soured cream
2 tbsp milk
1 mango, peeled, stoned and sliced
1 banana, peeled and sliced
1 star fruit, sliced
300 ml/½ pint double cream, whipped

◆

1 Base-line three 9 × 18 cm/3½ × 7 in loaf dishes with baking parchment.
2 Put the butter in a mixing bowl and cook on HIGH for 15 seconds to soften. Add the sugar and beat until light and fluffy. Beat in the eggs. Stir in 50 g/2 oz of the coconut, the flour, soured cream and milk and mix until well blended.
3 Divide the mixture between the dishes and spread evenly. Cook (one dish at a time) on HIGH for 2–2½ minutes, until springy to the touch and a skewer inserted into the centre comes out clean.
4 Leave to stand for 3 minutes, then turn out on to a wire rack to cool. Reserve half of the fruits for the decoration. Fold the rest into half of the cream and use to sandwich the cakes.
5 Spread the remaining cream round the sides and press the remaining coconut on to the cream. Arrange the rest of the fruit on top of the cake. Chill for 30 minutes, then cut into 10 slices.

From left to right: Mandarin sparkle, Tropical layer cake page 65

# MANDARIN SPARKLE

*Cook the puff pastry layers quickly by microwave, then hide their pale colour by brushing with a fruit juice glaze to make them golden and glossy. You can make the pastry layers in advance – they will freeze perfectly – but don't brush them with glaze until just before assembling or the pastry will become soggy.*

◆

700 g/1 ½ lb ready made puff pastry
3 × 300 g/11 oz cans mandarin orange segments in natural juice
2 tsp arrowroot
1 tbsp caster sugar
300 ml/½ pint double cream, whipped
2 tsp icing sugar

◆

1 Put a double layer of absorbent paper on 3 microwave racks.
2 Roll out the pastry on a floured surface to three 25 cm/10 in rounds. Prick all over and place one on each of the prepared racks. Chill for 15 minutes.
3 Cook (one at a time) on HIGH for 4½–6 minutes, until well risen and dry to the touch. Leave to stand for 5 minutes, then transfer to a wire rack to cool.
4 Drain the mandarin segments and pour 300 ml/½ pint of the juice into a jug. Cook on HIGH for 2 minutes. Blend the arrowroot and sugar with a little cold juice and stir into the hot juice. Cook on HIGH for a further 1½–2 minutes, until boiling and thickened, stirring 2 or 3 times.
5 Leave to cool slightly, then brush the rounds with the glaze. Chop one-third of the mandarin segments and fold into the cream with the icing sugar. Use to sandwich the pastry rounds together.
6 Arrange the remaining mandarin segments on top and brush with the remaining glaze. Serve at once, cut into 8–10 wedges.

# BLACK FOREST RING

◆

300 ml/½ pint milk
5 tbsp cocoa powder, sifted
115 g/4 oz butter
350 g/12 oz caster sugar
2 eggs, beaten
250 g/9 oz self-raising flour
pinch of salt
½ tsp baking powder
1 tsp vanilla essence
450 g/1 lb canned stoned red cherries
450 ml/¾ pint double cream, whipped
50 g/2 oz plain chocolate, coarsely grated

◆

1 Grease and base-line 2 deep 23 cm/9 in ring dishes.
2 Put the milk in a jug and cook on HIGH for 1½ minutes, then whisk in the cocoa powder and leave to cool.
3 Put the butter in a mixing bowl and cook on HIGH for 20 seconds to soften. Add the sugar and beat until light and fluffy, then beat in the eggs a little at a time, beating well after each addition.
4 Sift together the flour, salt and baking powder, then fold into the creamed mixture with the milk mixture and vanilla essence. Divide between the dishes.
5 Cook (one at a time) on HIGH for 7 minutes, or until springy to the touch and shrinking slightly from the sides of the dish. Leave to stand for 5 minutes, then turn out on to a wire rack to cool.
6 Drain the cherries and sprinkle 125 ml/4 fl oz of the juice over the sponges. Reserve 12 cherries and mix the rest into one-third of the cream and use to sandwich the cakes.
7 Spread all but 6 tbsp of the remaining cream over the top and sides of the cake. Press the chocolate over the sides, then pipe whirls of cream around the top edge and decorate with the reserved cherries. Cut into 12 slices.

# BRANDY AND WALNUT CAKE

*The brandy and walnuts used to flavour this recipe are a perfect combination and make the cake taste wonderful. However, the quantity of brandy in the icing means that it is definitely for grown ups only!*

◆

4 eggs
115 g/4 oz light soft brown sugar
25 g/1 oz butter
115 g/4 oz plain flour
1 tsp baking powder
225 g/8 oz shelled walnuts, chopped and toasted (see p. 120)
2 quantities Brandy Crème au Beurre (see p. 122)
icing sugar, to dust

◆

1 Grease and base-line 2 deep 20 cm/8 in round dishes.
2 Put the eggs and sugar into the bowl of an electric mixer and whisk until pale and mousse-like, and the mixture will hold a trail for 10 seconds. Put the butter in a small bowl and cook on HIGH for 1 minute to melt.
3 Sift together the flour and baking powder, then fold into the cake mixture with the butter and 150 g/5 oz of the walnuts. Divide between the prepared dishes and spread evenly. Cook (one at a time) on HIGH for 3 minutes, or until springy to the touch.
4 Leave to stand for 5 minutes, then turn out on to a wire rack to cook. Split the cakes horizontally. Make the butter cream and use half to sandwich the cakes together. Spread the rest over the top and sides.
5 Press the remaining walnuts over the top and sides of the cake and dust with icing sugar. Cut into 8–10 wedges.

## Lemon And Chocolate Layer

◆

4 eggs
115 g/4 oz caster sugar
115 g/4 oz self-raising flour
½ tsp baking powder
1 tbsp cocoa powder
1 tbsp hot water
grated rind and juice of ½ lemon
1 quantity Lemon Curd (see p. 119)
450 ml/¾ pint double cream, whipped
50 g/2 oz plain chocolate
1 lemon, finely sliced

◆

1 Grease and base-line two 15 × 23 cm/6 × 9 in dishes.
2 Put the eggs and sugar in the bowl of an electric mixer and whisk until pale and mousse-like, and the mixture will hold a trail for 10 seconds.
3 Sift the flour and baking powder 2 or 3 times, then fold into the mixture. Mix the cocoa and water to a smooth paste. Divide the cake mixture in 2, fold the lemon rind and juice into one part and the cocoa mixture into the other.
4 Spoon into separate dishes and spread evenly. Cook (one at a time) on HIGH for 2½–3 minutes. Leave to stand for 5 minutes, then turn out on to a wire rack to cool. Split the cakes in half horizontally.
5 Fold the lemon curd into the cream and use half to sandwich the cakes together, alternating the chocolate and lemon layers. Spread the rest over the top and sides.
6 Break the chocolate into squares, put in a small bowl and cook on MEDIUM for 2–3 minutes until melted, stirring once. Pour into a greaseproof paper piping bag, then drizzle in zig-zag lines over the cake.
7 Leave to set for 10 minutes, then decorate with lemon slices. Cut into 12 slices.

## Lime And Pineapple Gâteau

3 eggs
75 g/3 oz soft light brown sugar
75 g/3 oz wholewheat self-raising flour
5 ml/1 tsp baking powder
225 g/8 oz can pineapple pieces, drained
450 ml/¾ pint double cream, whipped
grated rind of 2 limes, plus 1 lime, thinly sliced to decorate
115 g/4 oz glacé pineapple

◆

1 Grease and base-line a deep 20 cm/8 in round dish.
2 Put the eggs and sugar in the bowl of an electric mixer and whisk until pale and mousse-like, and holding a trail for 10 seconds.
3 Sift the flour and baking powder two or three times and fold into the mixture with any bran caught in the sieve. Pour into the prepared dish and spread evenly. Cook on HIGH for 3–5 minutes, or until springy to touch.
4 Leave to stand for 5 minutes, then turn out on to a wire rack to cool.
5 Drain the pineapple and reserve the juice. Stir the pineapple into a third of the cream.
6 Split the cake horizontally and sprinkle with the reserved pineapple juice. Sandwich with the pineapple cream.
7 Flavour the remaining cream with the lime rind and spread over the sides and top of the cake. Decorate with the glacé pineapple and lime slices and chill until ready to serve. Serves 8–10.

# CREAMY STRAWBERRY SHORTCAKE

*Ordinary shortcake becomes very crumbly during microwaving so this version has a little extra flour and some water added to bind it together. Cut the top layer while it is still warm to make neat wedges.*

◆

175 g/6 oz butter
75 g/3 oz light soft brown sugar
225 g/8 oz plain flour, sifted
75 g/3 oz hazelnuts, chopped and toasted (see p. 120)
225 g/8 oz fresh strawberries
300 ml/½ pint double cream, whipped
8 shelled hazelnuts

◆

1 Line 3 baking trays with pieces of baking parchment.
2 Put the butter in a mixing bowl and cook on HIGH for 25 seconds to soften. Add the sugar and beat until light and fluffy. Stir in the flour, chopped nuts and 2 tbsp water and mix to a firm dough. Wrap in clingfilm and chill for 15 minutes.
3 Divide into 3 and roll out each piece on a floured surface to an 18 cm/7 in round. Place on the prepared baking trays and prick all over with a fork. Chill for 15 minutes.
4 Cook (one at a time) on HIGH for 3½–4 minutes, or until firm to the touch. Leave to stand for 5 minutes, then transfer to a wire rack to cool.
5 Cut one shortcake into 8 wedges with a sharp knife. Cut 4 of the strawberries in half and reserve for the decoration. Chop the rest and mix them into three-quarters of the cream. Use to sandwich the shortcakes, arranging the sliced round on top.
6 Pipe 2 whirls of cream on each wedge and decorate with the reserved strawberry halves and hazelnuts. Serves 8.

# TOFFEE NUT ROLL

◆

3 eggs
115g/4oz caster sugar plus extra for dusting
50 g/2 oz self-raising flour
pinch of baking powder
2 tbsp hot water
40 g/1½ oz blanched almonds, chopped and toasted (see p. 120)
500 ml/18 fl oz carton toffee fudge ice cream
75 ml/3 fl oz double cream

◆

1 Line a shallow 20 × 28 cm/8 × 11 in dish with baking parchment (or make a double case with baking parchment).
2 Put the eggs and sugar in the bowl of an electric mixer and whisk until pale and mousse-like, and the mixture will hold a trail for 10 seconds.
3 Sift together the flour and baking powder 2 or 3 times, then sift into the egg mixture. Gently fold in with the hot water and 25 g/1 oz of the almonds.
4 Pour into the prepared dish and tip the dish to make the mixture run into the corners. Cook on HIGH for 5–6 minutes, until springy and shrinking from the sides of the dish. Leave to stand for 3 minutes.
5 Place a sheet of baking parchment on the work surface and sprinkle with caster sugar. Turn the sponge out on to the sugared paper, carefully remove the lining paper and trim the edges of the sponge.
6 Lay another sheet of baking parchment on top and roll up from a short end; cool.
7 Cook the ice cream on LOW for 1 minute to soften. Leave to stand for 3 minutes. Unroll the sponge, remove the baking parchment, then spread the ice cream over the sponge. Roll up from one short side and wrap in baking parchment.
8 Freeze for at least 8 hours. To serve, pipe cream along top and sprinkle with remaining almonds. Cut into 12 slices.

Creamy strawberry shortcake, Toffee nut roll

**In** this section you will find cakes for special anniversaries and festive occasions that can all be made very speedily. There are marzipan-covered and iced light fruit cakes which, if soaked in brandy, can be made a week or so in advance, and cream or butter cream-coated light fruit cakes and sponge cakes that are best made on the day or at most the day before the party.

The recipes for Quick Birthday and Easter Cake are designed to be assembled at the last minute – vary the icing colours to suit the occasion and pipe a suitable message across the top.

The rich fruit Glazed Christmas Ring will keep for several days if wrapped tightly in foil, and is ideal for a small family – especially if you don't want to be eating Christmas cake for weeks after the festive season. There's no need to go to the trouble of icing it, the glittering colourful topping of nuts and glacé fruits makes it look fabulously festive. For a Christmas party, you can microwave the spectacular White Christmas Chocolate Cake. Coated and then filled with a rich white chocolate and cream mixture, it is simply, but very effectively, decorated with white chocolate holly leaves and berries. The recipe doesn't have to be reserved for Christmas – at other times of the year make the same cake, but use chocolate rose leaves to decorate it instead.

CHAPTER FIVE

# SPECIAL OCCASION CAKES

White Christmas chocolate cake

## WHITE CHRISTMAS CHOCOLATE CAKE

*Of all the cakes in this book, I like this one the best. It looks wonderful, tastes fantastic and has a huge number of calories per slice! I used white chocolate couverture, but Swiss chocolate or white chocolate bars will do just as well.*

◆

175 g/6 oz butter
175 g/6 oz caster sugar
3 eggs, beaten
150 g/5 oz white chocolate
1 tsp vanilla essence
3 tbsp hot water
200 g/7 oz self-raising flour, sifted
2 quantities White Chocolate Ganache (see p. 113)
20 White Chocolate Holly Leaves and Berries (see p. 121)
icing sugar, to dust

◆

1 Grease and base-line a deep 23 cm/9 in ring dish.
2 Put the butter in a mixing bowl and cook on HIGH for 25 seconds to soften. Add the sugar and beat until light and fluffy. Beat in the eggs a little at a time, beating well after each addition.
3 Break the chocolate into a small bowl and cook on MEDIUM for 3½–4 minutes to melt, stirring once. Stir into the creamed mixture with the vanilla essence, hot water and flour.
4 Spoon into the cake dish and smooth the surface. Cook on HIGH for 6½ minutes, or until springy to touch. Leave to stand for 10 minutes, then turn out on to a wire rack to cool. Split the cake horizontally.
5 Make the chocolate ganache and use one-third to sandwich the cake together. Spread the rest over the top and sides, leaving the surface very rough. Arrange the holly leaves and berries on top and dust with icing sugar. Cut into 16–20 slices.

## GLAZED CHRISTMAS RING

◆

225 g/8 oz butter
115 g/4 oz light soft brown sugar
5 eggs, beaten
250 g/9 oz plain flour
50 g/2 oz self-raising flour
1 tsp mixed spice
225 g/8 oz sultanas
50 g/2 oz currants
50 g/2 oz chopped mixed nuts
50 g/2 oz chopped mixed peel
75 g/3 oz glacé cherries, washed and dried
grated rind and juice of ½ orange
1 quantity Apricot Jam Glaze (see p. 124)
25 g/1 oz angelica
25 g/1 oz shelled Brazil nuts
25 g/1 oz blanched almonds
25 g/1 oz walnut halves

◆

1 Grease and base-line a deep 23 cm/9 in ring dish.
2 Put the butter in a mixing bowl and cook on HIGH for 30 seconds to soften. Add the sugar and beat until fluffy. Beat in the eggs a little at a time, beating well after each addition.
3 Sift the flours and spice into the mixing bowl. Add the sultanas, currants, chopped nuts and peel. Chop 50 g/2 oz of the cherries and add with the orange rind and juice.
4 Spoon into the dish and smooth the surface. Cook on HIGH for 5 minutes, then DEFROST for 10–15 minutes, or until firm to the touch and a skewer inserted into the centre comes out clean. Leave to stand for 15 minutes, then cool on a wire rack.
5 Make the apricot glaze and brush over the top and sides of the cake. Arrange the remaining glacé cherries, angelica, Brazil nuts, almonds and walnut halves on top and brush with the glaze. Leave to set for 30 minutes. Cut into 16–20 slices.

## EASTER CAKE

115 g/4 oz butter
225 g/8 oz caster sugar
3 eggs, beaten
115 g/4 oz plain flour
115 g/4 oz self-raising flour
115 g/4 oz sultanas
115 g/4 oz raisins
50 g/2 oz chopped mixed peel
150 g/5 oz glacé cherries, washed, dried and halved
50 g/2 oz glacé pineapple, chopped
125 ml/4 fl oz milk
125 ml/4 fl oz brandy (optional)
2 quantities Lemon Butter Cream (see p. 112)
20 Sugar Frosted Flowers (see p. 124)

1 Grease and base-line a deep 20 cm/8 in round dish.
2 Put the butter in a mixing bowl and cook on HIGH for 20 seconds to soften. Add the sugar and beat until light and fluffy. Add the eggs a little at a time, beating well after each addition.
3 Sift together the flours, then stir into the mixture with the dried fruit, peel, glacé fruit and milk and mix until well blended.
4 Spoon into the prepared dish and smooth the surface. Cook on HIGH for 5 minutes, then DEFROST for 20 minutes, or until a skewer inserted into the centre comes out clean. Leave to cool in the dish, then turn out.
5 Spoon the brandy over the cake, if using, and leave for a few minutes to soak in, then split the cake horizontally. Make the butter cream and use one-third to sandwich the cake together. Reserve 6 tbsp for piping and spread the rest over the top and sides, using a serrated edge scraper.
6 Pipe shells of butter cream round the top and bottom edges and decorate with the sugar frosted flowers. Cut into 12–16 wedges.

## CHRISTENING CAKE

115 g/4 oz butter
225 g/8 oz light soft brown sugar
3 eggs, beaten
115 g/4 oz plain flour
115 g/4 oz wholewheat self-raising flour
115 g/4 oz sultanas
115 g/4 oz raisins
115 g/4 oz chopped mixed glacé fruits
115 g/4 oz glacé cherries, washed, dried and quartered
125 ml/4 fl oz milk
125 ml/4 fl oz brandy (optional)
¼ quantity Apricot Jam Glaze (see p. 124)
icing sugar, to dust
450 g/1 lb marzipan
450 g/1 lb pink or blue Fondant Icing (see p. 118)
1 quantity pink or blue Royal Icing (see p. 118)
pink or blue ribbons and silk flowers, to decorate

1 Grease and base-line a deep 2.25 litre/4½ pint heatproof glass bowl.
2 Put the butter in a mixing bowl and cook on HIGH for 20 seconds to soften. Add the sugar and beat until light and fluffy. Add the eggs a little at a time, beating well after each addition.
3 Sift together the flours and stir into the mixture, tipping in any bran caught in the sieve. Stir in the dried and glacé fruits. Add the milk and mix until well blended.
4 Spoon into the prepared bowl and smooth the surface. Cook on HIGH for 5 minutes, then DEFROST for 20–25 minutes, or until a skewer inserted into the centre comes out clean. Leave to cool in the bowl, then turn out.
5 Spoon the brandy over, if using, and leave for a few minutes to soak in. Make the apricot glaze and brush over the cake. Dust a work surface with icing sugar and roll out the marzipan to a 25 cm/10 in circle. Use to cover the cake and trim round the bottom edge with a sharp knife.

6 Knead the fondant icing, then roll out and use to cover the cake as for the marzipan (brush the marzipan with a little brandy or egg white to help the icing stick). Place the cake on a cake board. Fill a small piping bag fitted with a star nozzle with royal icing and pipe shells round the bottom edge.
7 Make the ribbons and flowers into a small posy and fix on top of the cake with a little fondant or royal icing. Cut into 16–20 pieces.

## SILVER WEDDING BELL

*A bell-shaped cake is usually made in a metal tiffin mould available from cake decorating shops, but for microwaving a deep pudding basin works just as well. If the top is very flat, use some of the cake trimmings to round it off before covering with marzipan.*

◆

250 g/9 oz butter
250 g/9 oz light soft brown sugar
4 eggs, beaten
450 g/1 lb sultanas
grated rind and juice of 1 lemon
125 ml/4 fl oz brandy
350 g/12 oz plain flour
½ tsp mixed spice
¼ quantity Apricot Jam Glaze (see p. 124)
450 g/1 lb marzipan
450 g/1 lb white Fondant Icing (see p. 118)
silver and white ribbons and silk flowers, to decorate

◆

1 Grease and base-line a 1.75 litre/3 pint pudding basin.
2 Put the butter in a mixing bowl and cook on HIGH for 30 seconds to soften. Add the sugar and beat until light and fluffy. Beat in the eggs a little at a time, beating well after each addition.
3 Add the sultanas, lemon rind and juice and 1 tbsp of the brandy. Sift together the flour and spice and stir into the mixture until well blended. Spoon into the prepared basin and smooth the surface.
4 Cook on HIGH for 5 minutes, then DEFROST for 20–25 minutes, or until a skewer inserted into the centre comes out clean. Leave to cool in the bowl, trim the cake level with the edge of the basin, then turn out. Spoon the remaining brandy over the cake and leave for a few minutes to soak in.
5 Make the apricot glaze and brush over the cake. Dust a work surface with icing sugar and roll out the marzipan to a 23 cm/9 in circle. Use to cover the cake and trim neatly round the bottom edge with a sharp knife.
6 Knead the fondant icing until smooth, then use to cover the cake as for the marzipan (brush the marzipan with a little brandy or egg white to help the icing stick). Place the cake on a thin 10 cm/4 in cake board on top of a larger cake board.
7 Dust the work surface lightly with icing sugar and roll out the remaining fondant icing thinly. Use to make the frills; stamp out 8 rounds with a fluted 10 cm/4 in round cutter and remove the centre of each with a plain 2.5 cm/1 in cutter. Cover with clingfilm.
8 Take one ring at a time and roll the end of a wooden cocktail stick over the fluted edge until thin and puckered. Cut the ring, dampen the cake and carefully stick the frill on the cake, repeat with the other rings to make a double frill round the cake.
9 Make a spray with the ribbons and flowers and attach to the top of the cake with fondant icing. Cut into 20 pieces.

## VALENTINE CAKE

*I haven't found a heart-shaped microwave dish, but you can easily cut a square cake to the right shape. Let the sponge cool completely, then using a bread knife, and with a sawing movement, cut it neatly into a heart. The cut sides will be very crumbly, so spread with a thin first coat of cream to trap the crumbs before adding the final layer.*

◆

4 eggs
115 g/4 oz caster sugar
115 g/4 oz self-raising flour
1 quantity Sugar Syrup (see p. 120)
2 tbsp kirsch
225 g/8 oz strawberries, sliced
300 ml/½ pint double cream, whipped
½ quantity Redcurrant Jelly Glaze (see p. 124)

◆

1 Grease and base-line two 18 cm/7 in square dishes.
2 Put the eggs and sugar in the bowl of an electric mixer and whisk until pale and mousse-like, and the mixture will hold a trail for 10 seconds.
3 Sift the flour 2 or 3 times and fold into the mixture. Divide between the prepared dishes and spread evenly. Cook (one at a time) on HIGH for 2½–3 minutes, until springy to the touch. Leave to stand for 5 minutes, then turn out on to a wire rack to cool.
4 Using a paper template as a guide, cut each cake into a heart shape. Mix together the syrup and kirsch and sprinkle over the cakes; leave to soak in for a few minutes.
5 Stir 50 g/2 oz of the strawberries into half of the cream and use to sandwich the cakes together. Spread the remaining cream round the sides, then arrange the remaining strawberries on top, overlapping slightly. Make the glaze and brush over the strawberries. Leave to set for 15 minutes. Serves 8.

## QUICK BIRTHDAY CAKE

*Gone are the days when you could say you didn't have time to bake a cake! The 2 layers of this apricot-flavoured birthday cake take less then 5 minutes to cook – and with the help of your microwave, the flavouring and filling can be made in double quick time too.*

◆

115 g/4 oz dried apricots
175 g/6 oz butter
175 g/6 oz self-raising flour, sifted
175 g/6 oz caster sugar
3 eggs, beaten
2 tbsp milk
5 tbsp apricot jam
1 quantity Apricot Crème au Beurre (see p. 122)
¼ quantity Glacé Icing (see p. 114)
birthday candles

◆

1 Grease and base-line 2 deep 20 cm/8 in ring dishes.
2 Put the apricots and 3 tbsp water in a small bowl, cover and cook on HIGH for 4 minutes, stirring once. Leave to cool, then purée.
3 Put the butter in a mixing bowl and cook on HIGH for 25 seconds to soften. Add the flour, sugar, eggs, milk and apricot purée and beat until well blended. Divide the mixture between the dishes and smooth the surface.
4 Cook (one at a time) on HIGH for 4–5 minutes. Leave to stand for 5 minutes, then turn out and cool on a wire rack. Sandwich together with the jam.
5 Make the butter cream, reserve 8 tbsp and spread the rest over the top and sides of the cake. Put reserved 8 tbsp in a piping bag fitted with a star nozzle and pipe small stars round the top and bottom edges.
6 Put the glacé icing in a small greaseproof paper piping bag and pipe 'Happy Birthday' on top, then add the candles. Cut into 12–16 pieces.

## Garlic And Buttermilk Rolls

*Buttermilk is a slightly thickened milk with a pleasant tangy taste – during cooking, it helps the dough rise and keeps the rolls soft. Buttermilk was originally the sour milk left over from butter making, but now it is made from skimmed milk mixed with a culture. These rolls are great for picnics as they come ready buttered and break into neat little slices to eat.*

◆

500 g/1 lb 2 oz plain strong flour
½ tsp salt
¼ tsp bicarbonate of soda
1 sachet easy-blend yeast
400 ml/14 fl oz buttermilk
50 g/2 oz butter
1–2 garlic cloves, crushed
1 tsp light soft brown sugar
beaten egg, to glaze

◆

1 Grease the hollows of 2 bun trays.
2 Sift together the flour, salt and bicarbonate of soda into a mixing bowl. Stir in the yeast. Put the buttermilk in a jug and cook on HIGH for 1 minute. Put the butter and garlic in a small bowl, cover and cook on HIGH for 2 minutes.
3 Add the buttermilk, sugar and half of the garlic butter to the dry ingredients and mix to a soft, non-sticky dough. Knead for 5 minutes.
4 Place the dough in an oiled bowl, cover and cook on LOW for 4 minutes. Leave in a warm place to rise until doubled in size. Knock back, then cut in half and roll out each piece to a square about 3 mm/⅛ in thick.
5 Cut into strips about 4 cm/1½ in wide. Brush the strips with the remaining garlic butter and stack on top of each other, to make 2 separate stacks. Cut each stack crossways into 6 even-sized rectangles.
6 Keeping the layers together, turn the rectangular bundles on their sides and press into the hollows of the bun trays. Cook (one tray at a time) on LOW for 2 minutes, then leave to rise in a warm place until doubled in size.
7 Cook (one tray at a time) on HIGH for 2 minutes, or until springy to touch. Leave to stand for 5 minutes, then brush with the egg glaze and brown under a preheated grill. Serve warm. Makes 12.

## Poppy Seed Knots

*These pretty little rolls are ideal for a dinner party and are very quick to make because they are only left to rise once. After microwaving, they are quite white, but it is amazing what a little egg glaze, a sprinkling of poppy seeds and a quick browning under a grill can do.*

◆

550 g/1 ¼ lb packet white bread mix
beaten egg, to glaze
poppy seeds

◆

1 Grease 2 baking trays.
2 Make up the dough according to the instructions on the packet. Cut into 12 pieces and roll out each on a floured surface to a 15 cm/6 in sausage.
3 Tie the sausages into loose, single knots, keeping the ends short so that the rolls are as round as possible. Place 6 rolls in a circle on each of the baking trays.
4 Cook (one tray at a time) on LOW for 2 minutes, then leave in a warm place to prove until doubled in size. Cook (one tray at a time) on HIGH for 4–6 minutes.
5 Leave to stand for 5 minutes, then brush with the egg glaze and sprinkle with poppy seeds. Brown the tops under a hot grill, then wrap in a tea towel and leave to cool on a wire rack. Makes 12.

## MALTED TEALOAF

*Malt is a familiar taste in breakfast cereals and milky drinks. Jars of the syrupy malt extract can be bought in health food stores and a spoonful added to this mixture not only imparts a distinctive flavour but also, because malt is hygroscopic (which means that it holds moisture), makes the finished bread extra moist.*

◆

50 g/2 oz butter
115 g/4 oz golden syrup
115 g/4 oz malt extract
4 tbsp milk
225 g/8 oz wholewheat self-raising flour
pinch of salt
115 g/4 oz sultanas
50 g/2 oz chopped mixed peel
1 egg, beaten

◆

1 Grease and base-line a 900 g/2 lb loaf dish.
2 Put the butter, syrup, malt extract and milk in a bowl and cook on HIGH for 2 minutes to melt, stirring once. Leave to cool.
3 Sift the flour and salt into a mixing bowl, tipping in any bran caught in the sieve. Add the sultanas and peel, then mix in the melted mixture and egg and beat until smooth.
4 Pour into the dish and cook on MEDIUM for 10 minutes, then on HIGH for 3–4 minutes, or until springy to the touch and a skewer inserted into the centre comes out clean. Leave to stand for 5 minutes.
5 Turn out of the dish, wrap in a tea towel and cool on a wire rack. Cut into 12 slices.

## DATE AND WALNUT CAKE

*Tea bread, a cross between a cake and a bread, is often served sliced and spread with butter. This one is delicious served warm, so if you keep some until the next day, warm the slices in the microwave for a few seconds before spreading with butter.*

◆

350 g/12 oz self-raising flour
½ tsp salt
50 g/2 oz butter, diced
115 g/4 oz light soft brown sugar
50 g/2 oz chopped walnuts
115 g/4 oz stoned dates, chopped
1 tbsp black treacle
2 eggs, beaten
about 200 ml/7 fl oz milk

◆

1 Grease and base-line a deep 15 × 23 cm/6 × 9 in dish.
2 Sift the flour and salt into a mixing bowl, then rub in the butter until the mixture resembles fine breadcrumbs. Add the sugar, walnuts, dates, treacle, eggs and enough of the milk to mix to a soft dropping consistency.
3 Spoon into the dish and spread evenly. Cook on MEDIUM for 10 minutes, then on HIGH for 4–6 minutes, until springy to touch and just beginning to shrink from the sides.
4 Leave to stand for 5 minutes, then turn out. Wrap in a tea towel and leave to cool on a wire rack. Cut into 12 slices.

# Speedy Soda Bread

*This bread is very quick to cook – even by microwave standards – because its raising agent is bicarbonate of soda instead of yeast. It should have a soft floury crust, so wrap the cooked bread in a tea towel while it cools slightly, then split and spread with butter.*

450 g/1 lb wholewheat flour
2 tsp bicarbonate of soda
1 tsp salt
50 g/2 oz butter, diced
25 g/1 oz caster sugar
300 ml/½ pint milk
1 tbsp lemon juice

1 Grease a 25 cm/10 in round baking tray or plate.
2 Sift the flour, bicarbonate of soda and salt into a mixing bowl, tipping in any bran caught in the sieve. Rub in the butter until the mixture resembles fine breadcrumbs, then stir in the sugar.
3 Mix together the milk and lemon juice (the mixture will curdle) and add enough to the dry ingredients to mix to a soft, non-sticky dough.
4 Turn out on to a floured surface, knead very lightly, then pat out to a 18 cm/7 in round. Use a floured knife to cut a deep cross on the top. Dust with a little extra flour and transfer to the prepared dish.
5 Cook on MEDIUM for 8 minutes, then on HIGH for 2–4 minutes, until dry and springy to the touch. Leave to stand for 5 minutes, then cool on a rack, wrapped in a tea towel to keep the crust soft. Serve warm, broken into 4 large triangles.

# Blueberry Muffins

*Muffins are an American idea, where they're usually eaten warm for breakfast. Fresh blueberries are available in the summer and also at the very beginning of the year when they are imported from New Zealand. If unavailable, make the muffins with black or redcurrants instead.*

225 g/8 oz wholewheat flour
½ tsp baking powder
pinch of salt
50 g/2 oz light soft brown sugar
25 g/1 oz butter
1 tbsp honey
about 250 ml/8 fl oz milk
½ tsp bicarbonate of soda
175 g/6 oz fresh blueberries

1 Grease and base-line the hollows of 2 bun trays.
2 Sift the flour, baking powder and salt into a mixing bowl, tipping in any bran caught in the sieve. Stir in the sugar.
3 Put the butter and honey in a bowl and cook on HIGH for 1 minute to melt, then stir in the milk and bicarbonate of soda. Stir the butter mixture into the dry ingredients and beat until smooth, then stir in the blueberries.
4 Divide between the hollows of the bun trays and cook (one tray at a time) on HIGH for 3 minutes, or until springy to the touch. Leave to stand for 3 minutes, then wrap in a tea towel and leave to cool a little on a wire rack. Serve still warm, with butter and honey. Makes 12.

From left to right clockwise: Nutty-topped granary loaf page 92, Poppy seed knots page 83, Yorkshire teacakes

# YORKSHIRE TEACAKES

*These traditional yeast cakes are usually made quite large and would have to be microwaved one at a time. I've reduced the size so that they can be cooked 3 at a time. While they are still warm, brush the tops of the teacakes with a little honey or golden syrup to give them a sticky top.*

◆

300 ml/½ pint milk
450 g/1 lb strong plain flour
1 tsp salt
40 g/1½ oz white cooking fat
1 sachet easy-blend yeast
25 g/1 oz light soft brown sugar
115 g/4 oz currants
25 g/1 oz mixed chopped peel
beaten egg, to glaze

◆

1 Grease 3 baking trays.

2 Put the milk in a jug and cook on HIGH for 1 minute. Sift the flour and salt into a mixing bowl, rub in the fat, then stir in the yeast, sugar, currants and peel. Mix in enough of the milk to make a soft, non-sticky dough.

3 Knead for 5 minutes, then put into a large oiled bowl and cover. Cook on LOW for 4 minutes, then leave to rise in a warm place until doubled in size.

4 Knock the dough back, then divide into 9 pieces and roll each into a 10 cm/4 in round. Arrange 3 in a circle on each of the baking trays. Cook (one tray at a time) on LOW for 2 minutes, then leave to prove until doubled in size.

5 Cook (one tray at a time) on HIGH for 3 minutes, or until well risen and springy to touch. Leave to stand for 3 minutes, then brush with egg glaze and brown under a conventional grill. Wrap in a tea towel and cool slightly on a wire rack. Serve warm, split and spread with butter. Makes 9.

## APRICOT TEABREAD

*The flavours in this cake – apricot, orange and almond – blend together particularly well, and these ingredients also give the finished cake its rich golden colour. Do not add the sprinkling of chopped almonds until the cake has started to set or they will sink below the surface.*

◆

115 g/4 oz dried apricots, chopped
25 g/1 oz butter
225 g/8 oz caster sugar
275 g/10 oz wholewheat flour
pinch of salt
1 tsp bicarbonate of soda
1 egg, beaten
50 g/2 oz blanched almonds, chopped and toasted (see p. 120)
4–6 tbsp orange juice

1 Grease and base-line a 900 g/2 lb loaf dish.
2 Put the apricots, 150 ml/¼ pint water, butter and sugar in a bowl and cover. Cook on HIGH for 5 minutes, stirring once, then leave to cool.
3 Sift the flour, salt and bicarbonate of soda into a mixing bowl, tipping in any bran caught in the sieve. Stir in the apricot mixture, egg and half of the almonds, then beat in enough of the orange juice to make a soft dropping consistency.
4 Spoon into the prepared dish and smooth the surface. Cook on MEDIUM for 5 minutes, then sprinkle with the remaining almonds. Cook on MEDIUM for a further 3 minutes, then on HIGH for 2–3 minutes, until shrinking from the sides of the dish and a skewer inserted into the centre comes out clean.
5 Leave to stand for 5 minutes, then turn out, wrap in a tea towel and cool for about 30 minutes on a wire rack. Cut into 12 slices and serve, still slightly warm, spread with butter.

## OLD ENGLISH HERB BREAD

225 g/8 oz wholewheat flour
½ tsp salt
25 g/1 oz butter
1 tsp sugar
½ sachet easy-blend yeast
150 ml/¼ pint milk and water, mixed
1 tbsp chopped fresh parsley
1 tbsp chopped fresh thyme
175 g/6 oz Cheddar cheese, grated

1 Grease and base-line a deep 9 × 18 cm/3½ × 7 in dish.
2 Sift the flour and salt into a mixing bowl, tipping in any bran caught in the sieve. Rub in the butter, then stir in the sugar and yeast.
3 Put the milk and water in a small bowl and cook on HIGH for 30 seconds to warm, then add enough to the dry ingredients to make a soft, non-sticky dough. Knead for 5 minutes, then place in an oiled bowl and cover. Cook on LOW for 4 minutes. Leave in a warm place until doubled in size.
4 Knock back, cut into 3 pieces and roll out each one on a floured surface to fit the dish. Lay one piece in the dish.
5 Mix together the herbs and cheese and sprinkle one-third over the dough in the dish to within 5 mm/¼ in of the edge. Add a second layer of dough and cheese mixture, then top with the last piece of dough.
6 Push down the sides of the dough with the tips of your fingers so it domes slightly in middle. Cut a wide criss-cross pattern on the top with a sharp knife, then sprinkle with the remaining cheese and herbs.
7 Cook on LOW for 4 minutes, then leave in a warm place until the bread doubles in size. Cook on MEDIUM for 10 minutes, then on HIGH for 1–2 minutes, until it is

springy to the touch and just shrinking from the sides of the dish.
8 Leave to stand for 5 minutes, then turn out on to a wire rack to cool slightly. Serve warm, cut into 12–15 slices.

## Chocolate Chip And Raisin Buns

*This recipe makes 6 of these buns, but if that isn't enough, the recipe can easily be doubled or trebled. Cook extra buns in batches of 6. They are definitely best served warm while the chocolate drops are still melted.*

◆

115 g/4 oz wholewheat self-raising flour
½ tsp baking powder
pinch of salt
50 g/2 oz butter, diced
115 g/4 oz light soft brown sugar
25 g/1 oz rolled oats
25 g/1 oz raisins
25 g/1 oz plain chocolate drops
1 egg yolk
6 tbsp milk

◆

1 Grease and base-line the hollows of a bun tray.
2 Sift together the flour, baking powder and salt into a mixing bowl, tipping in any bran caught in the sieve. Rub in the butter until the mixture resembles fine bread-crumbs, then stir in the sugar, oats, raisins and chocolate drops.
3 Mix in the egg yolk and enough of the milk to make a soft, non-sticky dough. Divide the mixture between the hollows, leaving it rough, and cook on HIGH for 2–3 minutes, until springy to the touch.
4 Leave to stand for 3 minutes, then transfer to a wire rack to cool. Makes 6.

## Brown Crown Loaf

*This loaf is made up of separate balls of dough, arranged close together in a ring dish, so that as the bread rises they stick together. Once cooled, the bread easily breaks into soft triangular rolls. I have used strong brown flour, which has slightly less bran than wholewheat, and a pleasant malty taste – use half strong plain and half wholewheat instead, if preferred.*

◆

450 g/1 lb strong brown flour
½ tsp salt
15 g/½ oz white cooking fat
1 sachet easy-blend yeast
1 tbsp black treacle
2 tsp sesame seeds

◆

1 Grease and base-line a deep 23 cm/9 in ring dish.
2 Sift the flour and salt into a mixing bowl, tipping in any bran caught in the sieve. Rub in the fat, then stir in the yeast. Put 300 ml/½ pint water in a jug and cook on HIGH for 30 seconds until tepid. Stir in the treacle, then add enough of this mixture to mix to a soft, non-sticky dough.
3 Knead for 5 minutes, then place in an oiled bowl and cover. Cook on LOW for 4 minutes, then leave in a warm place until doubled in size.
4 Knock the dough back, then divide into 8 pieces. Roll into balls and place in the prepared dish. Brush the top with water and sprinkle evenly with sesame seeds. Cook on LOW for 4 minutes, then leave to prove in a warm place until level with the rim of the dish.
5 Cook on MEDIUM for 10 minutes, then on HIGH for 1–2 minutes, until just shrinking from the sides of the dish. Leave to stand for 5 minutes, then brown the top under a hot grill.
6 Wrap the bread in a tea towel and leave to cool on a wire rack. Serves 8.

## FIGGY BREAD

◆

350 g/12 oz wholewheat flour
½ tsp salt
75 g/3 oz butter, diced
25 g/1 oz caster sugar
1 sachet easy-blend yeast
125 ml/4 fl oz milk
1 egg plus 1 yolk, beaten
50 g/2 oz chopped walnuts
115 g/4 oz dried figs, finely chopped
50 g/2 oz light soft brown sugar
3 tbsp honey

◆

1 Grease and base-line a deep 15 × 23 cm/6 × 9 in dish.

2 Sift together the flour and salt, tipping in any bran caught in the sieve. Rub in half of the butter until the mixture resembles fine crumbs, then stir in caster sugar and yeast.

3 Put the milk in a jug and cook on HIGH for 30 seconds. Add the egg and yolk to the dried ingredients and mix in enough of the milk to make a soft non-sticky dough. Knead for 5 minutes.

4 Place in an oiled bowl and cover. Cook on LOW for 4 minutes, then leave to rise in a warm place until doubled in size. Knock back with your knuckles, then divide into 5 pieces and roll out each to fit the dish.

5 Put the remaining butter in a bowl, cook on HIGH for 1 minute to melt, then stir in the walnuts, figs, sugar and honey. Lay one piece of dough in the dish and spread with a quarter of the fig mixture. Repeat with the remaining dough and fig mixture, finishing with a layer of dough.

6 Cook on LOW for 3 minutes, then leave in a warm place to prove until doubled in size. Cook on MEDIUM for 9 minutes, then on HIGH for 2–4 minutes, until springy to touch and shrinking from the sides of dish.

7 Leave to stand for 5 minutes, then turn out and wrap in a tea towel. Leave to cool slightly on a wire rack. Cut into 16 slices.

## APPLE AND RAISIN TWIST

◆

225 g/8 oz strong plain flour
½ tsp salt
25 g/1 oz caster sugar
½ sachet easy-blend yeast
150 ml/¼ pint milk
25 g/1 oz butter
1 egg, beaten
150 g/5 oz raisins
1 eating apple, peeled, cored and thinly sliced
1 tsp cinnamon
1 tbsp demerara sugar

◆

1 Grease a round baking tray.

2 Sift together the flour and salt into a mixing bowl and stir in the sugar and yeast. Put the milk in a jug and cook on HIGH for 30 seconds until tepid. Put the butter in a small bowl and cook on HIGH for 1 minute to melt.

3 Add the butter, egg and enough of the milk to make a soft, non-sticky dough. Knead for 5 minutes, then place in an oiled bowl and cover. Cook on LOW for 3 minutes, then leave to rise in a warm place until doubled in size.

4 Knock the dough back, then work in 115 g/4 oz of the raisins. Cut in half and roll out each piece on a floured surface to a 35 cm/14 in sausage. Twist them together and form into a ring, pressing the ends together to join them. Place on the prepared tray.

5 Brush with a little milk and sprinkle with the remaining raisins and apple; press them into the dough. Mix the cinnamon and demerara sugar and sprinkle over the top.

6 Cook on LOW for 3 minutes; leave in a warm place until doubled in size. Cook on MEDIUM for 9 minutes, then on HIGH for 3–4 minutes, until springy to touch. Leave to stand for 5 minutes, then transfer to a wire rack. Cut into 12 slices.

From the top: Iced currant bread page 93, Figgy bread, Apple and raisin twist

## Oat And Onion Round

225 g/8 oz wholewheat flour
225 g/8 oz strong plain flour
½ tsp salt
1 sachet easy-blend yeast
250 g/9 oz rolled oats
25 g/1 oz light soft brown sugar
1 medium onion
50 ml/2 fl oz oil
175 ml/6 fl oz milk
25 g/1 oz butter

1 Grease and base-line a deep 20 cm/8 in round dish.
2 Sift the flours and salt into a bowl, tipping in any bran caught in the sieve. Stir in the yeast, 225 g/8 oz oats and sugar.
3 Cut half the onion into rings and reserve, chop the remainder finely and put in a bowl with the oil. Cover and cook on HIGH for 4 minutes to soften, stirring once, then add the milk and 175 ml/6 fl oz water.
4 Stir into the dry ingredients and mix to a soft dough. Knead for 5 minutes, then place in an oiled bowl, cover and cook on LOW for 4 minutes. Leave to rise in a warm place until doubled in size.
5 Knock back and knead lightly, pat into a round and drop into the prepared dish. Put the butter and onion rings in a small bowl, cover and cook on HIGH for 3 minutes to soften. Stir in the remaining oats and spread over the top of the loaf.
6 Cook on LOW for 4 minutes, then leave to prove in a warm place until doubled in size. Cook on MEDIUM for 10 minutes, then on HIGH for 3–4 minutes, until springy to the touch and just shrinking from the sides of the dish.
7 Leave to stand for 5 minutes, then turn out, wrap in a tea towel and cool on a wire rack. Cut into 10–15 slices.

## Nutty-Topped Granary Loaf

350 g/12 oz granary flour
25 g/1 oz white cooking fat
½ tsp salt
1 sachet easy-blend yeast
2 tsp black treacle
2 tbsp honey
15 g/½ oz cornflakes, crushed
25 g/1 oz chopped mixed nuts

1 Grease and base-line a 900 g/2 lb loaf dish.
2 Sift the flour into a mixing bowl, tipping in the bran and grains caught in the sieve. Rub in the fat, then stir in the salt and yeast. Put 200 ml/7 fl oz water and treacle in a jug and cook on HIGH for 30 seconds, until tepid.
3 Stir into the dry ingredients and mix to a soft, non-sticky dough. Knead for 5 minutes, then put in an oiled bowl and cover. Cook on LOW for 4 minutes, then leave to rise in a warm place until doubled in size.
4 Knock back with your knuckles, then roll out on a floured surface to a rough oblong as wide as the loaf dish is long. Roll up the dough from a short side and place in the loaf dish, seam side down.
5 Put the honey in a small bowl and cook on HIGH for 30 seconds. Stir in the cornflakes and nuts, mixing well, then spread over the top of the loaf. Cook on LOW for 4 minutes, then leave to prove in a warm place until doubled in size.
6 Cook on MEDIUM for 10 minutes, then on HIGH for 3–4 minutes, or until springy and shrinking from the sides. Leave to stand for 5 minutes, then wrap in a tea towel and cool slightly on a wire rack. Cut into 12 slices and eat warm.

# ICED CURRANT BREAD

◆

225 g/8 oz strong plain flour
1 tsp salt
25 g/1 oz butter, diced
½ sachet easy-blend yeast
25 g/1 oz caster sugar
50 ml/2 fl oz milk
1 egg yolk
50 g/2 oz currants
25 g/1 oz chopped walnuts
beaten egg, to glaze
½ quantity Glacé Icing (see p. 114)

◆

1 Grease and base-line a 900 g/2 lb loaf dish.
2 Sift the flour and salt into a mixing bowl. Rub in the butter until the mixture resembles fine breadcrumbs, then stir in the yeast and sugar.
3 Put the milk and 50 ml/2 fl oz water into a jug and cook on HIGH for 20 seconds, until tepid, then stir into the dry ingredients with the egg yolk, adding just enough of the milk mixture to make a soft, non-sticky dough.
4 Knead the dough for 5 minutes, then place in an oiled bowl and cover. Cook on LOW for 4 minutes, then leave in a warm place until doubled in size.
5 Knock the dough back with your fist, then add the currants and half of the walnuts and knead to mix them through the dough. Flatten the dough to a rough oblong, as wide as the loaf dish is long, and roll up from a short side.
6 Place the roll in the dish, seam-side down. Cook on LOW for 4 minutes, then leave to prove in a warm place until the top of the dough is about 1 cm/½ in above the rim of the dish.
7 Cook on MEDIUM for 8 minutes, then on HIGH for 1–3 minutes, until firm to the touch and shrinking slightly from the sides of the dish. Leave to stand for 5 minutes, then turn out. Brush the top with egg glaze and brown quickly under a hot grill. Wrap in a tea towel and cool on a wire rack.
8 Make the glacé icing and spread on top of the cake, letting a little trickle down the sides. Sprinkle with the rest of the walnuts, and leave to set. Cut into 12 slices.

# GOLDEN YEAST CAKE

◆

65 g/2½ oz butter
75 g/3 oz caster sugar
2 eggs, separated, plus 2 yolks
75 ml/3 fl oz milk
225 g/8 oz plain flour, sifted
½ sachet easy-blend yeast
grated rind of 2 lemons
few drops of vanilla essence
½ quantity Apricot Jam Glaze (see p. 124)

◆

1 Grease an 18 cm/7 in ring dish.
2 Put the butter in a mixing bowl and cook on HIGH for 15 seconds to soften. Add the sugar and beat until light and fluffy. Beat in the egg yolks a little at a time, beating well after each addition. Put the milk in a jug and cook on HIGH for 30 seconds.
3 Mix together the flour and yeast and stir into the creamed mixture with the lemon rind, vanilla essence and milk. Whisk the egg whites in a separate bowl with clean beaters until holding soft peaks, then carefully fold into the creamed mixture.
4 Pour into the prepared dish and cook on LOW for 3 minutes, then leave to stand in a warm place for 30 minutes.
5 Cook on HIGH for 8–10 minutes, until springy to the touch. Leave to stand for 5 minutes. Make the apricot glaze while the cake is standing, then turn it out on to a wire rack and brush with the glaze. Leave to set, then cut into slices. Serves 8–12.

**P**uddings microwave beautifully – steam puddings, either sponge or suet, work exceptionally well and are cooked in minutes rather than the hours required to steam them conventionally. For the suet recipes, look out for vegetable suet rather that the traditional beef; it's better for you, makes the puddings wonderfully light and gives them a less fatty taste.

Double crust pies, unfortunately, don't work in the microwave, the pastry stays soft and soggy while the filling overcooks. However, flan cases can be made quite easily and very successfully, as long as you follow a few simple rules. The pastry must be baked blind before being filled; it needs to be rolled thinly and evenly if it is to have a chance of becoming crisp; to keep the shape it should be chilled for 10–15 minutes before cooking, then lined with absorbent paper and filled with ceramic baking beans; and lastly, the case should be turned out of the dish and cooled on a wire rack – even if you are going to re-cook it later – so it stays as crisp as possible.

Baked cheesecakes microwave well too, either in a pastry flan case or on a crushed biscuit base. They need time to cool and set completely, but have a lovely creamy texture.

CHAPTER SEVEN

# PUDDINGS AND PIES

## TANGERINE TOWERS

*These little sponge puddings are served with a hot tangerine sauce. You can make an equally tasty store-cupboard version of the sauce using a small can of mandarin oranges in place of the tangerine rind and juice – but then they would really have to be called Mandarin Minarets!*

◆

150 g/5 oz butter
115 g/4 oz light soft brown sugar
2 eggs, beaten
½ tsp vanilla essence
2 tbsp grated tangerine rind
115 g/4 oz self-raising flour, sifted
3 tbsp milk
2 tbsp caster sugar
1 tbsp cornflour
150 ml/¼ pint tangerine juice
1 tbsp lemon juice

◆

1 Grease and base-line 6 paper cups and arrange in a circle on a baking tray.
2 Put 115 g/4 oz of the butter in a mixing bowl and cook on HIGH for 20 seconds to soften. Add the brown sugar and beat until light and fluffy. Beat in the eggs a little at a time, beating well after each addition.
3 Beat in the vanilla essence and half the tangerine rind, then stir in the flour and enough milk to make a soft dropping consistency. Divide equally between the cups and smooth the tops.
4 Cook on HIGH for 3–3½ minutes, until springy to touch. Meanwhile, prepare the sauce, mix the caster sugar and cornflour with a little of the tangerine juice, then stir in the rest of the tangerine juice, lemon juice, remaining butter and tangerine rind.
5 Cover the puddings and leave to stand for 3 minutes. Cook the sauce on HIGH for 2–3 minutes, until boiling and thickened, stirring 2 or 3 times. Turn the puddings out on to warm plates, pour the sauce around them and serve at once. Serves 6.

## SPICY PLUM UPSIDE-DOWN PUDDING

*This type of pudding cooks beautifully in the microwave, the fruit keeps its fresh flavour and its shape, and the topping becomes spongy and moist. Use drained canned stoned plums when fresh plums are out of season.*

◆

350 g/12 oz plums, halved and stoned
115 g/4 oz caster sugar
75 g/3 oz butter
75 g/3 oz light soft brown sugar
2 eggs, beaten
115 g/4 oz wholewheat, self-raising flour
½ tsp ground cinnamon
pinch of ground cloves
2 tbsp milk
cold Foamy Vanilla Sauce (see p. 119) or cream, to serve

◆

1 Grease a deep 18 cm/7 in round dish.
2 Put the plums, caster sugar and 3 tbsp water in a dish and cover. Cook on HIGH for 4–6 minutes, until tender, stirring 2 or 3 times. Leave to cool, then drain.
3 Put the butter in a mixing bowl and cook on HIGH for 15–20 seconds to soften. Add the brown sugar and beat until light and fluffy. Beat in the eggs a little at a time, beating well after each addition.
4 Sift together the flour and spices, then sift into the mixture, tipping in any bran caught in the sieve. Mix well, adding enough milk to make a soft dropping consistency.
5 Arrange the plums, cut side down, in the prepared dish and cover with the sponge mixture. Spread evenly, then cook on HIGH for 8–10 minutes, until springy to the touch. Leave to stand for 5 minutes, then invert on to a warm serving plate. Serve at once with the cold foamy vanilla sauce or cream. Serves 6.

## SUMMER FRUIT PUDDING

*I have a feeling that suet puddings are going to become fashionable again – the long steaming needed conventionally makes them impractical for today's lifestyle, but they can be microwaved in under 10 minutes and taste just as good, if not better. Keep the fillings fresh and light – this one has red summer fruits layered with the soft crumbly suet pastry.*

◆

75 g/3 oz self-raising flour
pinch of salt
75 g/3 oz fresh wholewheat breadcrumbs
75 g/3 oz shredded suet
115 g/4 oz caster sugar, plus extra
1 egg, beaten
about 3 tbsp milk
225 g/8 oz mixed redcurrants, raspberries and strawberries

◆

1 Grease and base-line a 15 cm/6 in soufflé dish.
2 Sift together the flour and salt. Stir in the breadcrumbs, suet and 50 g/2 oz of the sugar. Add the egg and enough of the milk to make a soft, non-sticky dough.
3 Turn out on to a floured surface and knead lightly. Cut the dough into 4 and roll out each piece to fit inside the dish. Slice any large fruits and mix them all with 50 g/2 oz of the sugar.
4 Place one round of dough into the dish and cover with a third of the fruit. Repeat the layers twice, then top with the last round of dough and press down gently.
5 Cover loosely with greaseproof paper, securing with fine thread, if necessary, and leaving a vent at the side for steam to escape. Cook on HIGH for 8–10 minutes, until firm to the touch and beginning to shrink from the sides of the dish. Leave to stand for 5 minutes, then turn out on to a warm dish. Sprinkle with sugar, cut into 6 wedges and serve with whipped cream.

## SAUCY FUDGE PUDDING

*This pudding doesn't look very pretty, but luckily it makes up for it in taste! It's made in an odd way – a milk and sugar mixture is poured over the sponge mixture before it is cooked – but magically, it turns into sponge pudding with a scrummy fudge sauce underneath. Children will love it.*

◆

115 g/4 oz butter
175 g/6 oz light soft brown sugar
1 egg, beaten
115 g/4 oz self-raising flour, sifted
450 ml/¾ pint milk
25 g/1 oz plain chocolate drops

◆

1 Grease and base-line a deep 20 cm/8 in round dish.
2 Put the butter in a mixing bowl and cook on HIGH for 20 seconds to soften. Add 115 g/4 oz of the sugar and beat until light and fluffy. Beat in the egg a little at a time, beating well after each addition.
3 Beat in the flour and enough of the milk to give a soft dropping consistency. Stir in the chocolate drops and spoon into the prepared dish. Put the remaining sugar and milk in a bowl and cook on HIGH for 2 minutes.
4 Pour the milk over the mixture in the dish and cook on HIGH for 8–10 minutes, until the top looks dry and the sauce begins to bubble round the edges. Leave to stand for 5 minutes, then serve at once. Serves 4.

Summer fruit pudding page 97

# SPOTTED DICK

*This currant pudding is another of the traditional desserts that I think will make a comeback with the microwave age. I've added equal quantities of wholewheat breadcrumbs and flour to make it really light and soft. Give it an appealing crumbly coating by sprinkling the inside of the bowl with crushed biscuits before you add the mixture.*

◆

15 g/½ oz butter
25 g/1 oz digestive biscuits, finely crushed
65 g/2½ oz light soft brown sugar
75 g/3 oz self-raising flour
pinch of salt
75 g/3 oz fresh wholewheat breadcrumbs
40 g/1½ oz shredded suet
175 g/6 oz currants
grated rind of ½ lemon
6 tbsp milk
1 quantity Foamy Vanilla Sauce (see p. 119)

◆

1 Thickly butter the inside of a 900 ml/1½ pint pudding basin. Mix together the biscuit crumbs and 15 g/½ oz of the sugar and press on to the buttery surface.
2 Sift the flour and salt into a mixing bowl. Stir in the remaining sugar, breadcrumbs, suet, currants and lemon rind and enough of the milk to make a soft dropping consistency. Spoon into the prepared basin and smooth the surface.
3 Make a wide pleat in a piece of greased grease-proof paper and use to cover the basin, securing with fine thread, if necessary, and leaving a vent at one side for steam to escape. Cook on HIGH for 6 minutes, or until firm to the touch.
4 Leave to stand for 5 minutes. Make the vanilla sauce and transfer to a warm jug. Turn out the pudding on to a warm plate and serve at once with the hot foamy vanilla sauce. Serves 6.

## CHRISTMAS PUDDING

*In the grand households in Victorian times Christmas puddings were cooked for an initial 6 or 8 hours, then reheated for a further 2–3 hours before serving. This recipe has a lighter texture and is ready to serve in about 35 minutes.*

◆

75 g/3 oz wholewheat flour
1 tbsp cocoa powder
1 tsp ground mixed spice
1 tsp ground cinnamon
½ tsp grated nutmeg
grated rind and juice of 1 orange
75 g/3 oz wholewheat breadcrumbs
50 g/2 oz light soft brown sugar
150 g/5 oz grated carrot
1 eating apple, peeled, cored and grated
50 g/2 oz shredded suet
115 g/4 oz raisins
75 g/3 oz currants
115 g/4 oz sultanas
75 g/3 oz stoned dates, chopped
2 tbsp black treacle
2 eggs, beaten
3 tbsp brandy
brandy butter, to serve

◆

1 Grease and base-line a 1.2 litre/2 pint pudding basin.
2 Put all the ingredients except half of the brandy and the brandy butter into a mixing bowl and mix well. Spoon into the prepared basin and smooth the surface. Make a wide pleat in a piece of greased greaseproof paper and use to cover the basin, securing with fine thread and leaving a vent at one side for steam to escape.
3 Cook on MEDIUM for 15 minutes, or until firm to touch; leave to stand for 5 minutes. Turn out on to a warm serving plate. Stick a piece of holly in the top, flame with the remaining brandy and serve with brandy butter. Serves 6–8.

## PEACH AND RASPBERRY CRUMBLES

*When fresh fruits are out of season you can make these individual puddings with frozen raspberries and canned peaches. Serve them hot with a dollop of cream or thick Greek yogurt on top.*

◆

115 g/4 oz caster sugar
350 g/12 oz fresh peaches, halved, stoned and sliced
225 g/8 oz fresh raspberries
75 g/3 oz plain flour, sifted
50 g/2 oz chopped toasted hazelnuts
115 g/4 oz muesli
50 g/2 oz light soft brown sugar
75 g/3 oz butter, diced

◆

1 Grease 4 individual heatproof dishes.
2 Put the caster sugar and 3 tbsp water in a shallow dish and cook on HIGH for 3–4 minutes, until the sugar has dissolved, stirring twice. Add the peaches, baste them with the syrup and cover.
3 Cook on HIGH for 4 minutes, or until tender, turning the peaches over and basting them halfway through the cooking time. Leave to stand for 5 minutes, then add the raspberries and set aside.
4 Put the flour, hazelnuts, muesli and brown sugar in a bowl and rub in the butter.
5 Spoon the fruit into the prepared dishes and sprinkle with the crumble mixture. Position the dishes in a circle and cook on HIGH for 5–7 minutes, until the crumble is cooked and the fruit bubbling, rotating the dishes a half turn once.
6 Leave to stand for 3 minutes, then serve at once. Serves 4.

# Bread And Butter Pudding

*This traditional pudding is one of my favourites. Conventionally it must be cooked in a bain-marie to keep the custard from over-cooking, but in the microwave it can be cooked to perfection on its own by using a low power. For the best result, choose an oval rather than round pie dish – its narrower, so the centre of the custard cooks and sets better.*

◆

50 g/2 oz butter
6 large slices wholewheat bread, crusts removed
75 g/3 oz pre-soaked dried apricots
grated rind of 1 lemon
3 eggs, beaten
3 tbsp light soft brown sugar
425 ml/15 fl oz milk
few drops of vanilla essence
1 tbsp demerara sugar

◆

1 Grease a 1.5 litre/2½ pint pie dish.
2 Put the butter in a small bowl and cook on HIGH for 15 seconds to soften. Spread butter on one side of the bread slices and cut each into 6 fingers. Arrange butter side up in the dish, layering them with the apricots and lemon rind.
3 Beat together the eggs and brown sugar until light and fluffy. Put the milk in a jug and cook on HIGH for 2 minutes. Beat the hot milk into the egg mixture and stir in the vanilla essence.
4 Pour over the bread and cook on MEDIUM for 15 minutes, or until just set. Cover and leave to stand for 5 minutes. Sprinkle with the demerara sugar and either serve at once or brown and crisp the top under a preheated grill. Serves 4.

# Cabinet Pudding

*This Victorian hot pudding is just as good – if not better – cold. Leave in a cool place for 2 or 3 hours after cooking so the flavours have a chance to mellow and blend together – then serve, cut in thin wedges with some pouring cream.*

◆

25 g/1 oz angelica, chopped
75 g/3 oz glacé cherries, washed, dried and quartered
25 g/1 oz sultanas
2 tbsp sherry
4 trifle sponges, cut into 1 cm/½ in cubes
12 ratafias or macaroon biscuits, crumbled
450 ml/15 fl oz milk
25 g/1 oz light soft brown sugar
3 eggs, beaten
few drops of vanilla essence

◆

1 Grease and base-line a 15 cm/6 in soufflé dish.
2 Soak the angelica, glacé cherries and sultanas in the sherry. Mix together the sponge cubes and three-quarters of the biscuit crumbs. Put half of the sponge cube mixture in the prepared dish, then add half of the fruit. Repeat the layers.
3 Put the milk in a large jug and cook on HIGH for 2 minutes. Whisk the sugar and eggs together until frothy, then pour on the milk, whisking all the time. Stir in the vanilla essence. Strain over the sponge, cover with greaseproof paper, securing with fine thread, if necessary, and leaving a vent at one side for steam to escape. Leave in a cool place to stand for 1 hour.
4 Cook on HIGH for 5 minutes, then on MEDIUM for 8 minutes, or until just setting in centre. Leave to stand for 5 minutes, then turn out on to a plate. Sprinkle with the remaining crumbs and either serve hot or leave to cool completely. Serves 6–8.

From the top: French apple flan, Pumpkin pie

## FRENCH APPLE FLAN

◆

115 g/4 oz plain flour
50 g/2 oz wholewheat flour
pinch of salt
1 tsp ground cinnamon
50 g/2 oz butter, diced
25 g/1 oz light soft brown sugar
1 egg, beaten
1 quantity Crème Pâtissière (see p. 114)
2 red apples, cored, halved and sliced
½ quantity Apricot Jam Glaze (see p. 124)
pouring cream, to serve

◆

1 Grease and base-line a 23 cm/9 in flan dish.
2 Sift the flours, salt and cinnamon into a mixing bowl, tipping in any bran caught in the sieve. Rub in the butter until the mixture resembles fine breadcrumbs. Stir in the brown sugar, egg and enough water to make a firm dough, about 2 tbsp.
3 Knead lightly, pat out to a 5 cm/2 in round, then wrap in clingfilm and chill for 15 minutes. Roll out on a floured surface to a 30 cm/12 in round. Use to line the dish, trim neatly and crimp the edge with fingertips. Chill for a further 15 minutes.
4 Prick all over and line with absorbent paper. Fill with ceramic baking beans and cook on HIGH for 4 minutes. Remove the beans and paper and cook for a further 1–2 minutes, until the base is dry. Leave to stand for 5 minutes, then invert on to a wire rack and leave to cool. When cold, return to the flan dish.
5 Make the crème pâtissière, pour into the case and spread evenly. Arrange the apple slices overlapping, in 2 or 3 circles on top. Cook on MEDIUM for 4 minutes, or until the apples are tender.
6 Leave to cool and set. Make the jam glaze and brush over the apple slices and pastry edge. Leave to set for 30 minutes. Cut into 6–8 wedges. Serve with cream.

## PUMPKIN PIE

*Americans make this pie around Thanksgiving Day when pumpkin is plentiful and it's almost the only way they eat it – even though it makes delicious soup, jam and sweet pickle.*

◆

175 g/6 oz wholewheat flour
pinch of salt
50 g/2 oz butter, diced
115 g/4 oz light soft brown sugar
1 egg yolk
450 g/1 lb cooked pumpkin, mashed
1 tsp ground cinnamon
150 ml/¼ pint single cream
3 eggs, beaten

◆

1 Grease and base-line a 25 cm/10 in flan dish.
2 Sift the flour and salt into a mixing bowl. Rub in the butter until the mixture resembles fine breadcrumbs, then stir in 25 g/1 oz of the sugar, the egg yolk and enough water to make a firm dough, about 3 tbsp.
3 Knead lightly, pat out to a 10 cm/4 in round, then wrap in clingfilm and chill for 15 minutes. Roll out on a floured surface to a 32.5 cm/13 in round. Use to line the dish, trim and crimp the edge with your fingertips. Chill for a further 15 minutes.
4 Prick all over with a fork and line with absorbent paper. Fill with ceramic baking beans and cook on HIGH for 4 minutes. Remove the beans and paper and cook for a further 1–2 minutes, until the base is dry. Leave to stand for 5 minutes, then invert on to a wire rack and leave to cool. When cold, return to the flan dish.
5 Put the pumpkin in a bowl and add the cinnamon, cream, eggs and remaining sugar. Mix well and pour into the pastry case. Cook on HIGH for 5 minutes, then on MEDIUM for 15 minutes, or until set in centre.
6 Leave to stand for 5 minutes, then either serve warm or cold. Serves 8–10.

## PRINCE ALBERT'S PUDDING

◆

130 g/4½ oz butter
350 g/12 oz prunes
grated rind and juice of 1 lemon
150 g/5 oz light soft brown sugar
2 eggs, separated
115 g/4 oz wholewheat breadcrumbs
40 g/1½ oz wholewheat semolina
1 quantity Foamy Vanilla Sauce (see p. 119)

◆

1 Use 15 g/½ oz of the butter to grease a 1.2 litre/2 pint pudding basin.
2 Put the prunes, grated rind and juice, 25 g/1 oz of the brown sugar and 300 ml/½ pint water in a bowl. Stir well, then cover and cook on HIGH for 12–15 minutes to soften, stirring twice.
3 Leave until cool, then drain. Halve and stone the prunes, then use about half of them to line the basin. Chop the rest.
4 Put the butter in a mixing bowl and cook on HIGH for 20 seconds. Add the rest of the sugar and beat until light and fluffy. Beat in the egg yolks a little at a time, beating well after each addition. Stir in the chopped prunes and lemon rind, the breadcrumbs and semolina.
5 Using clean beaters, whisk the egg whites in a separate bowl, until holding soft peaks, then fold into the mixture. Carefully spoon into the prune-lined basin and smooth the surface. Cover loosely with greaseproof paper, securing with fine thread, if necessary, and leaving a vent at the side for steam to escape.
6 Cook on HIGH for 10–12 minutes until the pudding is springy to the touch. Leave to stand for 5 minutes. Make the vanilla sauce, then invert the pudding on to a warm plate and serve at once with the sauce. Serves 6.

## STRAWBERRY SAVARIN

◆

115 g/4 oz wholewheat flour
pinch of salt
15 g/½ oz light soft brown sugar
½ sachet easy-blend yeast
125 ml/4 fl oz milk
2 eggs, beaten
50 g/2 oz butter
2 quantities Lemon Sugar Syrup (see p. 120)
1 quantity Foamy Vanilla Sauce (see p. 119)
225–275 g/8–10 oz fresh strawberries, quartered

◆

1 Grease an 18 cm/7 in ring mould.
2 Sift the flour and salt into a mixing bowl, tipping in any bran caught in the sieve. Stir in the sugar and yeast. Put the milk into a jug and cook on HIGH for 1 minute.
3 Stir the milk and eggs into the flour and beat vigorously for 5 minutes. Pour the mixture into an oiled bowl, cover and cook on LOW for 2 minutes and leave in a warm place for 20 minutes.
4 Put the butter in a small bowl and cook on HIGH for 20 seconds, then beat into the yeast mixture. Pour into the prepared ring mould and cook on LOW for 3 minutes. Leave in a warm place for 20 minutes.
5 Cook on HIGH for 7–9 minutes, until springy to the touch and just shrinking from the sides. Leave to stand for 5 minutes. Make the sugar syrup.
6 Turn out the savarin on to a wire rack over a large deep plate. Baste the warm savarin with the syrup until thoroughly soaked. Leave to cool.
7 Make the vanilla sauce, but don't whisk the egg whites yet. Leave the sauce to cool, stirring occasionally to prevent a skin forming then whisk the egg whites and fold into the cold sauce.
8 Put the savarin on a plate and fill the centre with the strawberries. Serve the foamy vanilla sauce separately in a bowl with a small ladle.

# Blackcurrant Cheesecake

*Ricotta is an Italian fresh white cheese made from either cow's or ewe's milk. In savoury dishes it's mixed with herbs to make pasta or pancake stuffings, but here it is sweetened and used as a smooth topping over blackcurrants and a biscuit crumb base.*

◆

75 g/3 oz butter
225 g/8 oz digestive biscuits, crushed
175 g/6 oz fresh blackcurrants
175 g/6 oz caster sugar
450 g/1 lb ricotta cheese
2 tbsp cornflour
2 eggs, beaten

◆

1 Grease and base-line a 20 cm/8 in flan dish.
2 Put the butter in a bowl and cook on HIGH for 1½–2 minutes to melt. Stir in the biscuit crumbs until well blended, then press two-thirds of the mixture into the base of the prepared dish.
3 Mix together the blackcurrants and 50 g/2 oz of the sugar and spread over the base. Put the cheese, remaining sugar, cornflour and eggs in a mixing bowl and beat well.
4 Carefully pour over the blackcurrants and spread evenly. Cook on MEDIUM for 12–15 minutes, until almost set in the centre. Sprinkle the remaining crumbs evenly over the top and leave to cool. Chill for at least 1 hour. Serves 8.

# Hampton Court Cheese Flan

*Curd and cottage cheese make a light creamy flan filling, flavoured with lemon and sultanas. The flan case is made of crushed biscuits – crush them finely, either in a food processor or place them in a polythene bag and roll over them several times with a rolling pin.*

◆

75 g/3 oz butter
225 g/8 oz digestive biscuits, crushed
2 eggs, beaten
75 g/3 oz caster sugar
225 g/8 oz curd cheese
175 g/6 oz cottage cheese
grated rind of 1 lemon
75 g/3 oz sultanas
grated nutmeg

◆

1 Grease and base-line a 20 cm/8 in flan dish.
2 Put the butter in a bowl and cook on HIGH for 1½–2 minutes to melt. Stir in the crumbs, mixing until thoroughly coated, then press on to the base and sides of the prepared dish. Cook on HIGH for 2 minutes, then leave to cool while preparing the filling.
3 Put the eggs and sugar in a mixing bowl and beat until pale and creamy. Beat in the cheeses and lemon rind, then stir in the sultanas. Pour into the crumb case.
4 Cook on HIGH for 3 minutes, then on DEFROST for 8–10 minutes, until almost set in the centre. Leave to cool, then chill for at least 1 hour. Sprinkle with the nutmeg, then cut into wedges. Serves 8.

Chocolate crumble cheesecake, Ginger and pineapple cheesecake page 108

# CHOCOLATE CRUMBLE CHEESECAKE

*This cheesecake has hazelnut and chocolate crumb mixture on the top and the bottom. Swirl the chocolate very lightly into the cheese mixture so the finished cheesecake is marbled and not all chocolate.*

◆

50 g/2 oz butter
225 g/8 oz plain chocolate digestive biscuits, crushed
115 g/4 oz chopped toasted hazelnuts
2 eggs plus 1 yolk, beaten
25 g/1 oz caster sugar
450 g/1 lb skimmed milk soft cheese
1 tbsp cornflour
150 ml/¼ pint double cream, whipped
115 g/4 oz plain chocolate

◆

1 Grease and base-line a deep 20 cm/8 in round dish.
2 Put the butter in a mixing bowl and cook on HIGH for 1½ minutes to melt. Add the biscuit crumbs and hazelnuts and stir together until the chocolate melts. Spread half the mixture in the base of the prepared dish and press down well with the back of a spoon.
3 Put the eggs, sugar, cheese and cornflour in a mixing bowl and stir well, then fold in the cream. Break the chocolate into squares and put in a small bowl. Cook on MEDIUM for 3–4 minutes to melt. Swirl into the cheesecake mixture and pour over the crumb base.
4 Cook on HIGH for 3 minutes, then on MEDIUM for 15–20 minutes, or until almost set in the centre. Sprinkle with the remaining crumbs and cook on MEDIUM for 5 minutes, then leave to cool. Chill for at least 1 hour before cutting into wedges. Serves 8.

## GINGER AND PINEAPPLE CHEESECAKE

◆

50 g/2 oz butter
50 g/2 oz light soft brown sugar
3 eggs plus 1 yolk
2 tbsp milk
50 g/2 oz self-raising flour
pinch of baking powder
1 tsp ground ginger
75 g/3 oz caster sugar
350 g/12 oz skimmed milk soft cheese
1 tbsp ginger syrup
425 g/15 oz canned pineapple pieces, drained
75 ml/3 fl oz double cream, whipped
2 pieces preserved stem ginger, thinly sliced
15 g/½ oz angelica, cut into small diamonds

◆

1 Grease and base-line an 18 cm/7 in cake or soufflé dish and also a 19 cm/7½ in sandwich dish.
2 Put the butter in a mixing bowl and cook on HIGH for 15 seconds to soften. Add the brown sugar, 1 egg and the milk. Sift in the flour, baking powder and ground ginger and beat until well blended.
3 Spoon into the sandwich dish and cook on HIGH for 2 minutes, or until springy to the touch. Leave to stand.
4 Separate the other two eggs and put the yolks in a bowl with the extra yolk and caster sugar. Beat until pale and creamy, then stir in the cheese and ginger syrup.
5 Finely chop half of the pineapple, drain well and add to the cheese mixture. Whisk the egg whites and fold in. Pour into the cake dish, cook on HIGH for 3 minutes, then on DEFROST for 8-10 minutes or until almost set in the centre.
6 Turn out the sponge and place on top of the cheesecake. Press down and leave to cool. Chill for at least 1 hour, then invert on to a plate. Decorate with cream, pineapple, stem ginger and angelica. Serves 6.

## APRICOT AND ORANGE TART

◆

115 g/4 oz plain flour
50 g/2 oz wholewheat flour
pinch of salt
50 g/2 oz butter, diced
25 g/1 oz light soft brown sugar
1 egg, beaten
1 quantity Thick Orange Custard (see p. 113)
½ quantity Apricot Jam Glaze (see p. 124)
1 orange, peeled and segmented
425 g/15 oz can apricot halves, drained

◆

1 Grease and base-line a 20 cm/8 in flan dish.
2 Sift the flours and salt into a mixing bowl, tipping in any bran caught in the sieve. Rub in the butter until the mixture resembles fine breadcrumbs. Stir in the brown sugar, egg and enough water to make a firm dough, about 2 tbsp.
3 Knead lightly, pat out to a 10 cm/4 in round, then wrap in clingfilm and chill for 15 minutes. Roll out on a floured surface to a 28 cm/11 in round. Use to line the dish, trim and crimp the edge with your fingertips. Chill for a further 15 minutes.
4 Prick all over and line with absorbent paper. Fill with ceramic baking beans and cook on HIGH for 4 minutes. Remove the beans and paper and cook for a further 1–2 minutes, until the base is dry. Leave to stand for 5 minutes, then cool on a wire rack. When cold, return to the flan dish.
5 Make the custard, pour into the case, spread evenly and cook on MEDIUM for 5 minutes. Leave to set. Make the glaze.
6 Arrange the orange segments in a ring round the edge of the custard filling. Cut the apricot halves in half from top to tail and arrange in the centre. Brush the fruit, custard and pastry edge with the glaze.
7 Leave to set, then cut into 6 wedges.

# Pecan And Passion Fruit Ring

*The dark purply skin of passion fruit becomes quite crinkly when the fruit is ready. To eat the fragrant seed-filled pulp straight from the shell, cut in half with a sharp knife and scoop out with a teaspoon. For flavouring desserts, rub the pulp through a fine nylon sieve to remove the seeds.*

◆

3 eggs, beaten
225 g/8 oz cream cheese
225 g/8 oz curd cheese
75 g/3 oz caster sugar
grated rind of 2 lemons
6–8 passion fruit
115 g/4 oz plain flour, sifted
50 g/2 oz butter, diced
50 g/2 oz shelled pecan nuts
50 g/2 oz light soft brown sugar

◆

1 Grease and base-line a deep 23 cm/9 in ring dish.
2 Put the eggs, cheeses, caster sugar and lemon rind in a bowl and beat together until well blended. Scoop out the flesh from 4 passion fruit and sieve into the cheese mixture.
3 Stir to blend, then pour into the prepared dish. Cook on HIGH for 3 minutes, then on MEDIUM for 5 minutes.
4 Put the flour in a mixing bowl and rub in the butter until the mixture resembles fine breadcrumbs. Stir in the pecan nuts, brown sugar and 2–3 tbsp water. Stir well to form a crumbly mixture.
5 Sprinkle over the cheesecake in an even layer and cook on MEDIUM for a further 6–8 minutes, until almost set. Leave to cool, then chill for at least 1 hour before turning out on to a serving dish.
6 Scoop out the flesh from the remaining passion fruit, spoon over the cheesecake and serve at once. Serves 8.

# Cherry Cheesecake

◆

115 g/4 oz plain flour
50 g/2 oz wholewheat flour
pinch of salt
50 g/2 oz butter, diced
25 g/1 oz light soft brown sugar
2 eggs
1 tbsp cornflour
50 g/2 oz caster sugar
5 tbsp plain fromage frais
300 ml/½ pint strained Greek yogurt
300 g/11 oz canned stoned red cherries

◆

1 Grease and base-line a 20 cm/8 in flan dish.
2 Sift the flours and salt into a mixing bowl, tipping in any bran caught in the sieve. Rub in the butter until the mixture resembles fine breadcrumbs. Stir in the brown sugar, 1 egg and enough water to make a firm dough, about 2 tbsp.
3 Knead lightly, pat out to a 10 cm/4 in round, then wrap in clingfilm and chill for 15 minutes. Roll out on a floured surface to a 28 cm/11 in round. Use to line the prepared dish, trim neatly and crimp the edge with fingertips. Chill for 15 minutes.
4 Prick all over and line with absorbent paper. Fill with ceramic baking beans and cook on HIGH for 4 minutes. Remove the beans and paper and cook for a further 1–2 minutes, until the base is dry. Leave to stand for 5 minutes, then cool on a wire rack. When cold, return to the flan dish.
5 Beat the remaining egg, cornflour and caster sugar in a bowl. Stir in fromage frais and half the yogurt. Drain the cherries and stir in half with 4 tbsp juice.
6 Pour into the pastry case and cook on HIGH for 3 minutes, then on DEFROST for 12–15 minutes, or until almost set in the centre. Leave to cool, then chill for at least 1 hour. Spread remaining yogurt over the top and decorate with cherries. Serves 6.

This chapter contains all the icings, fillings and decorations used in the recipes. Not all of them are microwaved, but they are essential for providing the finishing touches to microwaved cakes, biscuits and pies.

The microwave is invaluable for making sauces and custards and, once you have made them this way, I'm sure you will never cook them conventionally again: there's no bottom heat to make them catch; you can control the temperature so accurately, choosing a low power for delicate mixtures; and most need only an occasional stir or whisk to keep them perfectly smooth and lump free.

The microwave is also marvellous for melting chocolate for flavourings and decorations – mainly because there's no water involved. Even the tiniest amount of steam or water can cause chocolate to thicken and lose its gloss so the microwave is ideal for this job. It is much easier to melt tiny quantities of butter or gelatine in the microwave, or to toast nuts and coconut.

Sugar syrups and caramel are simple too, but these mixtures must be microwaved with extra care. They become extremely hot and will burn if cooked for even a few seconds too long – so keep a close watch. Remember that you can switch the microwave off and open the door at any time to check how quickly the mixture is cooking.

CHAPTER EIGHT

# ICINGS, FILLINGS AND DECORATIONS

## BUTTER CREAM

*This butter cream is much less sugary than the usual one made with icing sugar. Use unsalted butter or it will be unpleasantly salty. Take care when you boil the sugar syrup – microwave it in a heatproof bowl and check carefully during the cooking time because if it overheats, the sugar will caramelize.*

◆

75 g/3 oz caster sugar
2 egg yolks
115 g/4 oz unsalted butter
few drops of vanilla essence

◆

1 Put the sugar and 75 ml/3 fl oz water in a small heatproof jug and cook on HIGH for 2 minutes, then stir to dissolve the sugar. Cook on HIGH for a further 3–5 minutes, until the syrup will form a short thread between your finger and thumb.
2 Whisk the yolks while pouring on the syrup, then continue whisking until thickened and cool. Put the butter in a small bowl and cook on HIGH for 20 seconds to soften.
3 Whisk in the egg mousse a little at a time, then whisk in the vanilla essence.

**Variations**

*Coffee:* Add 2 tsp instant coffee dissolved in 2 tsp boiling water.
*Orange, lemon or lime:* Omit the vanilla essence and add the grated rind of 1 orange or lemon, or 2 limes.

## FRANGIPANE CREAM

*This thick almond flavoured cream is used as a cake or flan filling.*

◆

1 tbsp plain flour
1 tbsp cornflour
3 tbsp caster sugar
200 ml/7 fl oz milk
2 egg yolks
40 g/1 ½ oz ground almonds
75 ml/3 fl oz double cream, whipped

◆

1 Sift the flours into a bowl, add the sugar and 2 tbsp of the milk and mix to a thick paste. Whisk in the egg yolks.
2 Put the remaining milk in a jug and cook on HIGH for 1½ minutes. Whisk into the yolk mixture, then strain back into the jug. Cook on MEDIUM for 2½–3½ minutes, until boiling and very thick, whisking 2 or 3 times.
3 Leave to stand for 3 minutes, whisking occasionally, then cover the surface with clingfilm to prevent a skin forming.
4 Leave until cold, then fold in the ground almonds and cream. Use at once. Makes 450 g/1 lb, sufficient to fill a 20 cm/8 in cake or 6 individual pastry cases.

## CHOCOLATE GANACHE

*This blend of whipped cream and chocolate sets slightly on cooling and makes a wonderful filling and covering for both plain and chocolate cakes. It can be made with plain, milk or white chocolate.*

75 g/3 oz chocolate
25 g/1 oz caster sugar
300 ml/½ pint double cream, whipped

1 Break the chocolate into squares and put in a small bowl. Cook on MEDIUM for 4–5 minutes, until melted, stirring once.
2 Stir in 3 tbsp water and the sugar and cook on MEDIUM for 3 minutes, or until thickened, stirring once. Leave to cool, stirring occasionally.
3 Fold in the cream. Use at once. Makes about 425 ml/¾ pint, sufficient to fill and top a 20 cm/8 in cake.

## THICK VANILLA CUSTARD

*This is a good economy version of Crème Pâtissière (see p. 114) and can be substituted in all the recipes. It can be made without the whipped cream, but the cream makes it very light and soft.*

2 tbsp custard powder
2 tsp caster sugar
300 ml/½ pint milk
50 ml/2 fl oz double cream, whipped
few drops of vanilla essence

1 Put the custard powder and sugar in a bowl. Stir in 2 tbsp of the milk and blend to a smooth paste.
2 Put the remaining milk in a jug and cook on HIGH for 2 minutes, then pour on to the custard powder mixture and stir well.
3 Cook on HIGH for 2–3 minutes, until boiling and thickened, stirring 2 or 3 times. Cover the surface with clingfilm and leave to cool.
4 Fold in the cream and vanilla essence and use at once. Makes about 425 ml/¾ pint, sufficient to fill a 20 cm/8 in pastry case.

**Variations**

*Orange, lemon or lime:* Omit the vanilla essence and add the grated rind and juice of 1 orange or lemon, or 2 limes.

## CRÈME PÂTISSIÈRE

*This egg custard is mainly used as a flan filling. It's thickened with a mixture of flour and cornflour so you must make sure it boils for at least a minute to cook the flour, otherwise it may taste raw. Flavour the custard as you like, substituting other essences or grated citrus rind for the vanilla essence.*

◆

2 eggs, beaten
50 g/2 oz caster sugar
25 g/1 oz plain flour
25 g/1 oz cornflour
300 ml/½ pint milk
few drops of vanilla essence

◆

1 Put the eggs and sugar into a bowl and whisk until pale and creamy. Sift in the flours and whisk until well mixed.
2 Put the milk in a jug and cook on HIGH for 2 minutes. Pour on to the egg mixture, whisking all the time. Whisk in the vanilla essence.
3 Cook on HIGH for 2–2½ minutes, until thickened, whisking 2 or 3 times. Cover the surface with clingfilm and leave to cool.
4 Use at once or keep in an airtight container for 1–2 days. Makes about 425 ml/¾ pint, sufficient to fill a 20 cm/8 in pastry case.

## GLACÉ ICING

*A simple uncooked icing that is used for coating biscuits and cakes. It ought to be the easiest icing to make, but in my experience it is quite tricky to get the right consistency – if it is too thin it will run off. You must add the water drop by drop, mixing well after each addition, until the icing is just thick enough to find its own level in the bowl (when a trail made with a fork disappears after a second or two).*

◆

225 g/8 oz icing sugar, sifted
few drops of food colouring (optional)

◆

Sift the icing sugar into a bowl and stir in just enough water to make a smooth icing that just finds its own level in the bowl, about 5–6 tsp. Add a few drops of colouring, if wished. Use at once.

### Variations

*Orange, lemon or lime:* Use citrus juice instead of water – the juice will colour the icing a pale pastel so there's no need to add any colouring.
*Honey and lemon:* Add 2 tsp honey and 2–3 tsp lemon juice in place of the water.
*Coffee:* Add 2 tsp instant coffee granules to 2 tsp boiling water and use in place of some of the cold water.
*Chocolate:* Add 2 tsp sifted cocoa powder to the icing sugar before mixing with the water.
*Ginger:* Add 3 tsp ginger syrup in place of 3 tsp of the water.

Strawberry and custard slices page 28

## CARAMEL FROSTING

*This cooked frosting is very soft at first, then firms up as it cools. If it hardens too much before you have time to spread it, cook on HIGH for a few seconds, then beat well. It can be kept in an airtight container for several weeks but will need to be softened as above before spreading.*

◆

50 g/2 oz butter
115 g/4 oz light soft brown sugar
2 tbsp milk
few drops of vanilla essence
225 g/8 oz icing sugar, sifted

◆

1 Put the butter and brown sugar in a bowl and cook on HIGH for 2–3 minutes to melt. Stir in the milk, vanilla essence and icing sugar and beat well.
2 Leave in a cool place for 5–10 minutes, until firm enough for spreading, then use at once. Makes 400 g/14 oz, sufficient to fill and cover an 18 cm/7 in square cake.

## CHOCOLATE FUDGE FROSTING

*Use this soft, rich frosting for plain or chocolate cakes. It looks most effective if you leave the surface in rough peaks or large swirls.*

◆

225 g/8 oz plain chocolate
115 g/4 oz butter
2 eggs, beaten
350 g/12 oz icing sugar, sifted

◆

1 Break the chocolate into squares and put in a bowl with the butter. Cook on MEDIUM for 4 minutes, or until melted, stirring once or twice.
2 Beat in the eggs and sugar and leave in a cool place for 10–20 minutes, until thick enough for spreading, stirring occasionally. Use at once. Makes 700 g/1½ lb, sufficient to fill and cover an 18 cm/7 in cake.

## FROMAGE FRAIS FROSTING

*Fromage frais is a light, low-fat soft cheese that makes a lovely soft frosting.*

50 g/2 oz butter
4 tbsp fromage frais
few drops of vanilla essence
225 g/8 oz icing sugar, sifted

1 Put the butter in a bowl and cook on HIGH for 1 minute to melt. Stir in the fromage frais, vanilla essence and icing sugar, then beat well.
2 Leave in a cool place for 5–10 minutes, until firm enough for spreading.

**Variations**

*Orange, lemon or lime:* Omit the vanilla essence and add the grated rind of 1 orange or lemon, or 2 limes.
*Cream cheese:* For a richer, slightly thicker frosting, substitute cream cheese for the fromage frais.
*Strawberry:* Substitute strawberry flavoured fromage frais.

## FAST FROSTING

*Frosting a microwave cake can be a little tricky. Because the cake has no firm crust, the crumbs get into the frosting which can look untidy. So if the cake has a very soft texture, apply a thin first coat while the frosting is still slightly warm, then spread on a second thicker coat once the frosting has thickened.*

50 g/2 oz butter
2 tbsp milk
450 g/1 lb icing sugar, sifted
few drops of vanilla essence

1 Put the butter in a bowl and cook on HIGH for 1 minute to melt. Stir in the milk, icing sugar and vanilla essence, then beat until smooth.
2 Leave in a cool place for 3–10 minutes, until thick enough for spreading. Makes 450 g/1 lb, sufficient to fill and coat an 18–20 cm/7–8 in cake.

**Variations**

*Orange, lemon or lime:* Omit the milk and vanilla essence, add the grated rind of ½ orange or lemon, or 1 lime, and 2 tbsp of the juice.
*Chocolate:* Add 2 tbsp sifted cocoa powder with the icing sugar.

## FONDANT ICING

*This dual-purpose icing can be used in 2 different ways. Once mixed, it is a smooth pliable icing that can be rolled out as a cake covering either on its own or over marzipan, or it can be melted with a little water and spooned over sponge cakes to give a thin smooth coating.*

◆

2 tsp powdered gelatine
2 tbsp liquid glucose
2 tsp glycerine
450 g/1 lb icing sugar
1 tsp lemon juice
few drops of food colouring (optional)

◆

1 Put 2 tbsp water in a small bowl and sprinkle the gelatine over the top. Leave to soak for 10 seconds, then cook on HIGH for 30–45 seconds until hot. Stir to dissolve the gelatine.
2 Add the glucose and glycerine and cook on HIGH for a further 30 seconds to warm through.
3 Sift the icing sugar into a mixing bowl, add the gelatine mixture and lemon juice and mix with a wooden spoon until the mixture begins to bind together.
4 Turn out on to a work surface lightly dusted with icing sugar. Knead until smooth, kneading in a little food colouring, if wished.
5 Wrap tightly in clingfilm and keep in a cool place, but not the refrigerator, until required. Makes 700 g/1½ lb, sufficient to cover a 20–23 cm/8–9 in cake.

## ROYAL ICING

*Small quantities of royal icing are best mixed by hand. Use a palette knife so that you don't beat in too much air. It needs to hold firm peaks for piping, so if the icing is too soft, add a little more sifted icing sugar. If it is too firm, add a few drops of water. The glycerine isn't essential, but it keeps the icing from getting too hard.*

◆

1 egg white
¼ tsp lemon juice
225 g/8 oz icing sugar, sifted
½ tsp glycerine
few drops of food colouring (optional)

◆

1 Put the egg white and lemon juice in a bowl and beat lightly with a palette knife.
2 Add the icing sugar a little at a time, beating with the palette knife, until it will form fine, pointed peaks.
3 Stir in the glycerine and food colouring, if wished. Place the icing in an airtight container, cover the surface with clingfilm then cover with the lid. Leave to settle for at least 30 minutes before using. Makes 225 g/8 oz.

## FOAMY VANILLA SAUCE

*This sauce is equally good hot or cold, but if it is to be served cold, cover the surface with clingfilm at the end of step 3 and leave to cool. Whisk the egg whites and fold into the cold sauce just before serving.*

300 ml/½ pint milk
1 vanilla pod, split
2 eggs, separated
2 tbsp caster sugar

1 Pour the milk into a jug, add the vanilla pod and cook on HIGH for 2 minutes. Cover and then leave to infuse for 10–15 minutes.
2 Discard the vanilla pod and cook on HIGH for 1½–2 minutes, until almost boiling. Whisk the egg yolks and sugar until pale and creamy, then whisk in a little of the hot milk.
3 Strain back into the rest of the milk and cook on HIGH for 2 minutes, or until thickened, stirring every 30 seconds.
4 Whisk the egg whites in a clean bowl until holding soft peaks, then whisk into the custard. Cook on HIGH for 1 minute, then pour into a serving jug. Makes about 300 ml/½ pint.

## LEMON CURD

*This tangy preserve, gets its flavour from the fresh lemon – make sure you grate all the rind from the lemon and grate it directly into the bowl so you trap the zest that sprays out. Then cook the lemon on HIGH for 30 seconds before you cut and squeeze it – it yields a lot more juice when it is warm.*

115 g/4 oz caster sugar
50 g/2 oz unsalted butter
1 egg plus 1 egg yolk, beaten
grated rind and juice of 1 lemon

1 Put the sugar, butter, egg and yolk and lemon rind and juice in a bowl and cook on MEDIUM for 8–10 minutes, or until thick, whisking every minute for 5 minutes, then every 30 seconds.
2 Pour into sterilized jars, cover and leave to cool and set. Makes about 225 g/8 oz. Keeps for 2–3 weeks in the refrigerator.

## PRALINE

*These caramel and almond flavoured crumbs are used as a cake decoration or as a crunchy flavouring for cream or butter cream. Crushing the praline is easiest done in a food processor, but you can crush it by hand – break the praline into lumps, place in a strong polythene bag and roll over it several times with a rolling pin.*

◆

50 g/2 oz shelled almonds
50 g/2 oz caster sugar

◆

1 Brush a small baking tray with oil.
2 Put the almonds, sugar and 2 tbsp water in a small heatproof bowl and cook on HIGH for 8–10 minutes, until turning a pale caramel, stirring once or twice.
3 Using oven gloves to pick the bowl up, immediately pour on to the prepared tray in a thin layer. Leave until hard, then crush to a fine powder. Makes 115 g/4 oz quantity, sufficient to coat the sides of a 20 cm/8 in cake.

## SUGAR SYRUP

*This light syrup can be used either for fruit salad or for sprinkling over cakes to make them extra moist. If liked, flavour the syrup by adding a few thick strips of orange, lemon or lime rind, a vanilla pod, or a bay leaf while it is cooking and cooling.*

75 g/3 oz caster sugar
citrus rind, vanilla pod or bay leaf (optional)

1 Put the sugar, 150 ml/¼ pint water and the flavouring, if using, in a jug and cook on HIGH for 1–2 minutes, until boiling, stirring 2 or 3 times to dissolve the sugar.
2 Cook for a further 2 minutes, then leave to cool. Remove the flavouring when cool. Makes 150 ml/¼ pint, sufficient for a fruit salad for 4, or to moisten 2 or 3 layers of cake. Store any extra in a screw-top jar in a cool place, it will keep for several weeks.

## TOASTED COCONUT AND NUTS

*Because of their high fat content desiccated coconut and nuts will brown in the microwave when they are cooked on their own. They brown more quickly and evenly if cooked in a microwave roasting bag: spread the coconut or nuts in a thin even layer and shake the bag frequently to distribute the heat. Remember to handle the bag with oven gloves because it will be very hot. If you don't have a roasting bag just spread out the coconut or nuts on a plate and cook for a minute or so longer than the time given here, stirring several times.*

115 g/4 oz desiccated coconut, or chopped or flaked nuts

1 Put the coconut or nuts in a roasting bag and tie loosely with a non-metal tie.
2 Spread out evenly and cook on HIGH for 4–8 minutes, shaking the bag every minute at first, then every 30 seconds as they begin to brown. Makes 115 g/4 oz quantity.

**Note:** It isn't a good idea to cook very tiny amounts of food in the microwave, so this is the smallest quantity that you can safely toast. If the recipe calls for ½ quantity, make the full 115 g/4 oz amount and use the rest in other recipes. You can, however, increase the ingredients, but they will take longer; for instance, 225 g/8 oz will take 6–10 minutes to brown.

## CHOCOLATE DECORATIONS

*Plain chocolate is dark and rich and when mixed with other ingredients gives a good strong flavour. Milk and white chocolate can be used too, although they have a much milder taste and give a softer result. Chocolate-flavoured cake covering can also be substituted – it doesn't have as good a flavour, but it is much cheaper. You can turn chocolate into wonderful cake decorations, everything from the easy cut-out shapes to the more difficult long thin rolls called caraque.*

◆

115 g/4 oz chocolate

◆

1 Break the chocolate into squares and place in a small bowl. Cook on MEDIUM for 3–4 minutes until soft, then stir until melted and smooth. Use as required:

## CHOCOLATE SHAPES

◆

1 Spread the chocolate in a thin even layer on a piece of foil or waxed paper. Leave until just set.
2 Cut into squares, diamonds or triangles using a sharp knife and a ruler, or stamp out rounds using a small cutter.

## PIPED CHOCOLATE DECORATIONS

◆

1 Put the chocolate in a small paper piping bag, snip off the end and pipe shapes or squiggles on to foil or waxed paper. Leave to set, then peel off the paper.

## ROSE OR HOLLY LEAVES

◆

1 Pick fresh undamaged leaves and wash and dry thoroughly. Brush the veined underside with a thin layer of melted chocolate and leave to set, chocolate side up, on foil or waxed paper.
2 Brush with a second coat of chocolate and leave to set again. When firm, carefully peel off the leaves.

## CHOCOLATE CARAQUE

◆

1 Pour the chocolate on to a marble slab or other cool work surface and spread thinly. Work the chocolate back and forth using a palette knife until it begins to set and lose its gloss. Leave until just set.
2 Pull a knife, held at a slight angle, across the chocolate with a slight sawing movement to scrape off long thin rolls or short curls.

# Caramel Shapes

*These little decorations are very easy to make, so don't just keep them for cakes, they also make a fun decoration for ice cream and other desserts. Watch the caramel mixture very carefully while it cooks because it can easily burn. Remember that it will continue cooking for a short time after you switch off the microwave. Use oven gloves because the jug will get very hot.*

◆

75 g/3 oz caster sugar

◆

1 Place a sheet of baking parchment on a baking tray.
2 Put the sugar and 3 tbsp water in a small heatproof jug and cook on HIGH for 1–2 minutes or until boiling, then stir to dissolve the sugar.
3 Cook on HIGH for a further 3–4 minutes until pale golden. Leave to cool and thicken slightly, then dip a small spoon in oil, and use to drizzle the caramel in thin squiggly lines on to the baking parchment to make 24 similar shapes.
4 Leave until hard, then peel off the paper. Makes 24.

# Crème au Beurre

*This velvety smooth butter cream is made with a thin egg custard that can be flavoured in lots of different ways. Make sure the custard is completely cool before beating into the butter; if it is too warm, the butter will melt making the crème au beurre too soft for spreading.*

◆

75 g/3 oz caster sugar
3 egg yolks
5 tbsp milk
few drops of vanilla essence
175 g/6 oz unsalted butter

◆

1 Put the sugar and egg yolks in a bowl and whisk until pale and frothy. Whisk in the milk and cook on MEDIUM for 2½–3 minutes, until thick enough to coat the back of a spoon, whisking after 1 minute then every 30 seconds.
2 Stir in the vanilla essence, then cover the surface with clingfilm to prevent a skin forming and leave to cool.
3 Put the butter in a small bowl and cook on HIGH for 25 seconds to soften. Beat well, then gradually beat in the custard. Use at once or keep in an airtight container in a cool place for up to a week. Makes 350 g/12 oz, enough to fill and cover a 20 cm/8 in cake.

**Variations**

*Apricot:* Omit the vanilla essence and beat in 2 tbsp sieved apricot jam with the custard.
*Brandy:* Add 3 tbsp brandy with the vanilla essence.
*Coffee:* Stir 1 tbsp instant coffee granules into the custard before cooling.
*Orange, lemon or lime:* Omit the vanilla essence and add the juice and grated rind of 1 orange or lemon, or 2 limes to the custard.

Coffee and caramel gâteau page 65, decorated with Caramel shapes

# JAM OR JELLY GLAZE

*These versatile glazes, are not only used to coat fruit toppings on pies and cakes, but are also useful for brushing cakes to trap stray crumbs before covering with marzipan or icing. You can use any type of jam or jelly – although redcurrant and apricot are the most popular. The glazes look most effective on fruits of the same or a similar colour.*

◆

5 tbsp jam or jelly
1 tbsp lemon juice

◆

1 Put the jam or jelly in a small bowl with the lemon juice and 1 tbsp water. Cook on HIGH for 1½–2 minutes, until boiling, stirring occasionally.
2 Sieve jam glaze to remove seeds or chunks of fruit while still hot, then use the jam or jelly glaze while still warm.
3 Keep any extra in a small jar in the refrigerator – it will keep for several weeks. Makes about 5 tbsp, sufficient to coat the fruit in two 20 cm/8 in pies.

# SUGAR FROSTED FLOWERS

*Small flowers and petals make very pretty decorations for cakes and desserts. They can be preserved by coating them in sugar and drying quickly in the microwave. Not all flowers can be used though, as some are quite poisonous – edible flowers include borage, clover, daisies, marigolds, nasturtiums, violets and primroses.*

◆

about 24 flower heads or petals
a little lightly beaten egg white
1 tbsp caster sugar

◆

1 Wash and dry the flowers carefully, then brush them with a thin layer of egg white.
2 Sprinkle them with sugar, then brush with more egg white and sprinkle once more with sugar.
3 Arrange them in a circle on a piece of absorbent paper and cook on DEFROST for 4–5 minutes, or until almost dry, turning them over halfway through.
4 Leave in a warm dry place until completely dry and crisp. Place them in a box, layered with absorbent paper, and store in a dry place.

# INDEX

## D



## E



## F